ETHEL MANNIN

AN ITALIAN JOURNEY

HUTCHINSON OF LONDON

HUTCHINSON & CO (Publishers) LTD
3 Fitzroy Square, London W1

London Melbourne Sydney Auckland
Wellington Johannesburg Cape Town
and agencies throughout the world

First published 1974
© Ethel Mannin 1974

Set in Monotype Fournier
Printed in Great Britain by The Anchor Press Ltd
and bound by Wm Brendon and Son Ltd
both of Tiptree, Essex

ISBN 0 09 121460 2

For
Antony Hayes
who arranged it all, and made it all possible,
in friendship and deep gratitude

CONTENTS

ILLUSTRATIONS

ACKNOWLEDGMENTS

My gratitude is due to John Greenwood, Press Officer of the Italian State Tourist Office, London, for his patience and perseverance in obtaining for me photographs I specially wanted for this book; to Antony Hayes for photographs, and travel assistance of every kind; and to my old friend 'Tim' (F.W.) Ziemsen for assistance with proofs.

I am indebted, also, for information and illuminative comment, to the authors of the three books I took with me on my journey: the invaluable *Blue Guide to Northern Italy* (Benn), Hugh Honour's *The Companion Guide to Venice* (Collins), and James Morris's *Venice* (Faber), to all of which I had recourse when writing this book, and would urge all travellers to Venice and Northern Italy to include in their baggage.

E. M.

I

TO VENICE THE 'HARD' WAY

FROM London you can fly to Venice in two hours; or you can go what is nowadays considered the 'hard' way, by boat and train, leaving London at three-thirty in the afternoon and reaching Venice in the evening of the following day.

The 'hard' way is in fact a pleasant and interesting journey – the night train from Calais, and in the morning and afternoon of the next day a journey through Switzerland and the Simplon Tunnel into Italy, with mountains and lakes a great part of the way.

I went the 'hard' way, faithful to my vow of November, 1966, when I flew back from Damascus – having flown out – that henceforth I was grounded. Not that there was anything wrong with that Syrian flight, but simply that there comes a point when you feel that if you traipse about any more along that boutique half-mile on Rome airport, looking at all those large boxed dolls, and waiting, waiting for your 'plane to take off again, you will go mad. Enough is enough. So, having flown quite extensively, to Russia, the USA, the Far East – Tokyo, Rangoon – the Middle East – Cairo, Amman, Jerusalem, Damascus, Kuwait – I was grounded in 1966. For good. For good in all senses, for it is good to *travel* – as opposed to being merely transported, like cargo.

My journey to Venice in the autumn of 1973 was not, in fact, hard at all, but, on the contrary, very soft, for, thanks to the good friend to whom this book is dedicated – and who was very keen that I should write it – I had a sleeper from Calais and on arrival in Venice a reservation at that most distinguished of hotels, the Gritti Palace, on the Grand Canal. My last visit to Venice had been in the spring of 1964, when I was travelling by Greek steamer to Alexandria, en route to Cairo, and I sat up all night, second class, from Calais; which was a hard thing. So that nearly ten years later it was very agreeable – shall we say? – to be travelling soft; and having done a good deal of really tough journeying in my time I was truly grateful. I am not first-class orientated in any direction; in general it is not my 'scene'; but to reject the generously offered hospitality of a friend would be churlish, and in this particular circumstance – since I was set on making the journey – plain silly.

I was worried about the Gritti, though. How would the likes of me fit in? I demanded. I hadn't the clothes. I hadn't the right ideas, background, social what-nots. What sort of people stayed at the Gritti, anyway? Anyhow, not *my* kind! Grandeur was strictly not my line. There were *pensioni* galore in Venice – much more 'me'. It was agreed that there were many very good *pensioni* in Venice, but it was also pointed out that the cheapest of the good ones would cost me not less than four pounds a day, *demi-pension*, whereas the Gritti would cost me nothing at all. The point, really, was that I could hardly afford *not* to stay there. It was also explained to me that the Gritti Palace was not 'grand'. Nothing so vulgar. It was, simply, an impeccably good hotel. Quietly, unostentatiously good. As to the people who stayed there, they would obviously have to be fairly well-heeled, but also they would be people with a taste for good manners and elegance, in addition to the obvious things such as comfort and good food. As to the food it was, of course, as impeccable as all else; the smoked salmon, I was assured, was flown in from Scotland . . . which, of course, was a great relief (otherwise one might have been fobbed off with that pale pink Canadian stuff – mightn't one, I mean?) and one way and another I decided that perhaps, after all, the likes of me *could* stay in the Gritti and *like* it. *Quietly* good; unostentatiously *de luxe*. Yes, I would like that.

Journeys commonly begin at airports, seaports, or railway stations. Mine began at Victoria, which, in the days before air-travel took over, proudly proclaimed itself the 'gateway to Europe'. It began on a bright, sunny afternoon in late September, 1973, with the apples ripening in the orchards as the train ran through Kent. On the train were a great many young people with enormous packs on their backs. In the corner opposite sat a girl with a long flowing skirt, clumpy shoes like black clogs, long, synthetic blonde hair which she continually brushed back; her bosom fairly well exposed; heavy eye-shadow but no lipstick. All the way to Folkestone she sat absorbed in Cervantes' *Extraordinary Tales*.

The interior of the boat was raucous with non-stop relayed pop music, inescapable even on deck. People were queuing at a self-service counter for tea and coffee and sandwiches. The sea was flat and blue, with gulls wheeling, and the white cliffs receding but still visible when the French coast came into view, making the idea of the Channel Tunnel suddenly seem feasible – though still not desirable. Desirable, it seemed in the bright sunshine, to be an island – a piece of land entirely surrounded by water, as we learned at school. No porters at Calais, but it is not far to the train, and a porter at the entrance to the *wagons-lits* relieves me of the typewriter and bag. I settle into the compartment and drink the brandy and ginger-ale and eat the sandwiches, with which I have provided myself. Dinner is available, but since, according to a card tucked into a rack on the wall, *petit déjeuner*, consisting of tea or coffee *complet*, is six francs – ten to the pound sterling at the current rate – I wonder what can be the price of dinner. But I am well enough with my own provisions, and relaxed now that the small difficulties of the journey are behind me, but tired, and glad to turn in – the attendant having made up the bed – before we reach the deserted station of Amiens soon after nine.

We reach Paris at ten-thirty, and there is the always exciting glimpse of the floodlit Sacré Cœur at the top of Montmartre. We make the circle to the Gare de Lyon, and there are people trudging along beside a *wagon-lit* carrying handgrips and paper carriers, and a girl pushing a trolley with luggage, and night and loneliness and desolation are over everything. I draw down the blind and lie down and resume attention to Brian Moore's novel, *The Lonely Passion of Judith Hearne*, in which I do not entirely believe, but which makes, as they say, compelling reading.

The next I know there are lights along a river, and a high-rise block, and the time is two-forty, and it is Dijon.

With me night-journeys pass very quickly, for I have that oddity that I can sleep anywhere except in a bed. I can sleep in trains and 'planes and on 'buses, at concerts and theatres and cinemas, so that the wheels turning under me in a berth on a train present no problem. Are even soporific. So that the next I know it is seven-thirty and Montreux, and the lovely Lake of Geneva, and memories of the thirties, of being here with people close to me and dear to me – 'in other worlds – long ago'.

But there is the shock of a high-rise tower beside the lake. *Pollution* rears its hideous head. Even in Switzerland. Then the reassurance of the ancient Château of Chillon. There are shabby old apartment houses with balconies and a clutter of zinc baths and rickety cane furniture, and washing, and outcrops of scarlet geraniums gaily defying squalor.

Then it is St Maurice, and mountains, and toylike chalets, and the flat green fields of the valleys, and, winding down the window, the air is cold and fresh. Switzerland!

The *petit déjeuner*, ordered the night before, comes at eight, and, surprise, surprise, the coffee is 'instant', likewise the milk. There are two slices of white bread, rather dry, in a cellophane packet, a portion of butter, wrapped, a small carton of strawberry jam, an orange, two biscuits in a cellophane bag, a triangle of cheese. There is a red plastic jug of hot water, and a red plastic cup. All very hygienic and modern, and not very nice; but in the circumstances welcome.

Sion soon after that, with some ugly buildings, but apple orchards and vineyards at each side of the Rhône, intensive cultivation, very orderly and precise, almost regimented, and at nine o'clock Visp, with a large car park, a high rise hotel, pylons; Visp of all those happy Swiss memories of the thirties – the 'little village of Visp', of which I wrote so lyrically in *Privileged Spectator* in 1938, and where my daughter, Jean, and I had been together so happily in May, 1936, on our way up to Zermatt, breaking in our new climbing boots. Ah well, it is nearly forty years ago now; things change. It's just a pity that they so seldom change for the better.

Well, then, so that was Visp, and half an hour later it is Brig, or Brigue, and the Simplon Tunnel, and it will be good to plunge into that darkness, for from Visp on all has been industrialization and ugliness and modern blocks, and finally the Queen Victoria Hotel.

1921 is spelled out in huge figures over the entrance arch to the tunnel. We enter it at nine-fifteen and at nine-thirty we are in Italy, at Iselle di Trasquera. Since the tunnel was opened in 1906 I wonder why it says 1921 over the arch of the entrance at Brig. *N'importe.* I only wondered.

There are snowcapped mountains when we emerge, but the bright Swiss day has clouded over. There is half an hour's wait at Domo-dóssola, which we leave at eleven o'clock Italian time. We come to Stresa and Lake Maggiore, which I have never seen before, and I am astonished by its beauty; I have known the Swiss lakes and the Austrian lakes and the English lakes, but this, with the mountains rising sheer from it, is something different. Staggering.

We stay by Lake Maggiore for some time, but when we leave it all is drear. The approach to Milan is flat and ugly and feature-less. There are roads streaming with cars and lorries there are waste grounds and rubbish dumps and an unutterable drear.

The train arrives on time in Milan and I am met by a very charming young man who says his name is Giovanni, and who is very anxious to be helpful, to get me food and drink, and to be assured that I am all right. He escorts me to the train for Venice, and I look forward to meeting him again at Milan in a few weeks' time. The journey from Milan to Venice is desperately dull, through a completely featureless landscape, and the rain which had threatened as soon as we emerged into Italy from the Simplon Tunnel has now set in in earnest.

The station before Venice proper is called Venice-Mestre, about

B

which something should be done, for it confuses tourists, some of whom alight at it, instead of at Santa Lucia. Mestre is the dreadful industrial mainland suburb of Venice – a source of livelihood for the young of Venice, and a source of the pollution which contributes to the destruction of the ancient city. I do not know the answer. Nor, really, does anyone else.

I arrived in Venice in pouring rain, and the train was half an hour late. The rain had apparently set in on the Sunday evening – it was by then Tuesday evening – and had never let up. The railway station of Venice is near the Piazzale Roma, where there is a multi-storey car park accommodating two thousand five hundred cars. There are modern office blocks here, and a 'bus terminal. As an introduction to the 'white swan of cities', the most unique and fantastic of cities, it leaves everything to be desired. But then so does the approach by railway bridge and motor road across the lagoon from the mainland.

And yet – as soon as you have extricated yourself from the crowd on the Piazzale Roma and crossed the few yards to the Grand Canal none of all that matters. At the water's edge despite the crowds and the commotion of traffic it is *Venice*, the undoubted queen. I was met, and escorted to a motor-launch, and even in the rain, with heavy grey skies over, the Grand Canal, with ornately beautiful palaces at either side, is not less than superb, and in a few minutes the launch was rocking and roaring at the bobbing landing-stage of one of the smaller and less ornate palaces, the Palazzo Gritti, which had been the residence of the doge, Andrea Gritti, in the sixteenth century, and since 1948 one of the world's most beautiful and distinguished hotels. That I might ever stay there had never remotely occurred to me – it was not my 'scene', for one thing, and for another I could not possibly have afforded it.

But it proved to be not all as I had expected – and feared; that is to say the rooms were not dark and stately and haunted by American tycoon types; the elegance was of a quite different order, and the clientele youngish – mainly American, but quiet. The Gritti is altogether quiet. Quietly elegant. Even in the bar, which opens on to the terrace, the music of the piano is only part of a soft, general ripple of chatter and laughter.

My room was white and gold, with a massive crystal chandelier, and facing across to the floodlit beauty of the church of Santa Maria della Salute. And there was a bottle of Möet and Chandon in a bucket of ice on a marble-topped chest, with the compliments of the friend who had arranged it all, and a handsome vase of carnations with the compliments of the management.

I dealt immediately with the bottle in the bucket. What was all the fuss about?

A few notes about the Gritti and those who have stayed there are perhaps of some interest.

There is an Ernest Hemingway apartment and a Somerset Maugham apartment. Hemingway reputedly wrote his novel, *Across the River and into the Trees* there in 1948. According to an article in *Gourmet, the Magazine of Good Living,* for February, 1973, the Gritti's head housekeeper, Signora Cosima Giandomenici (she was named after Wagner's widow, he having died in Venice, and the signora's parents having been ardent Wagnerians) found Hemingway 'a sweet man' – which is anyhow a new angle on this aggressive and alcoholic American he-man. He had, she said, 'such *dolce*, soft eyes', and he would ring for caviar and champagne every morning at ten, and then would follow 'an enormous quantity of Valpolicella red wine', and 'later there would be whisky'. He would sit up in bed, propped up against the pillows, with the windows open, and write whilst looking out on to the canal, the signora told Joseph Wechsberg, the writer of the article. (It sounds like Mr Hemingway had himself a good stay at the Gritti, and that such daily consumption would build up to a sizable hangover. . . .) Anyhow, the novel got written, and in it he makes his Colonel hero refer to the Gritti as 'the best hotel in a city of great hotels', thus earning it a place in literature.

On the same floor Maugham also wrote whilst looking out on to the Grand Canal – though how any author could write in a room overlooking so noisy a thoroughfare, with the windows open, beats me; but perhaps it was less noisy, because of less motor-traffic then, and there were only the cries of the gondoliers under the windows, not the chug of motor-launches. Maugham was a regular visitor to the Gritti, almost to the end of his life; he went every summer, and always had the same suite – now known as the Maugham suite – and he liked the flowers that decorated it to be red carnations. According to an article in *The New York Times*, April 15, 1973, Signora Giandomenici recalled that Maugham would sit doing *petit point* embroidery whilst his secretary read to him, and that 'a strong scent of Schiaparelli's "Shocking" pervaded the apartment'. Whether he had *dolce* eyes, like Hemingway, the signora does not say, nor what he drank, though it is on record that he liked that small, amiable Italian white wine, Soave, with his dinner, and was apparently always pleased that the wine-waiter remembered that he liked it and had it waiting for him in the ice-bucket, year after year. Which is the quintessence of that personal touch in service upon which the Gritti prides itself.

The celebrities who have stayed at the Gritti form a *Who's Who* of the literary, film, and social world. More interesting is that Ruskin wrote part of *The Stones of Venice* there, and that Dickens, George Sand, and Wagner were there. Perhaps it was less expensive in those days. Well, almost certainly. It has only been the super-elegant *de luxe* hotel it is today since 1948. It was the home of the 67th doge of Venice, Andrea Gritti, in the last years of his life, and was the residence of the Gritti family as late as the eighteenth century. When the rising tide of tourism overtook Venice it became an annexe to the great Grand Hotel – which is now a government office, which seems a sad waste of a handsome building – on the Grand Canal. As as annexe the palace of the Grittis became run-down, until it was rescued in 1947 by CIGA, the Campagna Italiana Grandi Alberghi, the official Italian hotel chain, and severed its undistinguished ties with the Grand Hotel. CIGA remodelled the poor old palazzo and made it the 'jewel and showplace of its collection of luxury hotels'. The exterior remained in its original state, but the interior had to be entirely remodelled, to modernize it as a mid-twentieth-century hotel without destroying its character as the palatial residence of the sixteenth-century Doge. All the rooms were furnished with originals or reproductions of Renaissance antiques, original oil paintings, massive gilded mirrors, fabulous chandeliers of Venetian crystal; the rugs on the marble floors were Oriental, the curtains to the deep windows of heavy brocade. Lamps from seventeenth-century Venetian galleons light the corridors, and on the first floor there is a ceiling by Tiepolo. With all this was combined air-conditioning throughout; and there is television only in the suites. The hotel staff is considered the best in Venice.

The Doges' Suite, on the first floor, facing on to the canal, costs 100,000 lire a night, that is to say about £80. What dinner costs I have no idea, and, since Continental breakfast costs the equivalent of £1, would rather not know. But you cannot fault either the food or the service; the service is immaculate, and the food, whether it is a speciality such as chicken à la Gritti, or sole *primo amore*, or simply roast beef and Yorkshire pudding, is all that the proper combination of good food and good cooking should be. Dr Natale Rusconi, the managing director, personally examines each day's consignments of fish, meat, vegetables, fruit, rejecting a crab here, a prawn there, and when it comes to his daily inspection of the rooms with Signora Giandomenici frowning at a flower arrangement here, a piece of upholstery there. Of such meticulous attention to detail is a great hotel made – and the Gritti is one of the world's great hotels, though in size one of the smallest of the great hotels, with only 101 rooms, including ten suites, and even at the height of the season the staff of 125 outnumbers the guests.

Outside of the dining-room, and for the room-service waiter who promptly brings whatever you have telephoned for, you are remarkably unaware of staff. I never set eyes on a chambermaid, and in the corridors you are spared those squalid heaps of used sheets piled outside the rooms of departing guests which commonly affront one, even in first-class hotels, everywhere. But the Gritti is something very much more than a first-class hotel; it is the Palazzo Gritti, with all the refinement, elegance and beauty implied. You do not, for example, wait for the lift in a corridor, but at one end of a beautiful *salle* with paintings, massively gilded mirrors, fine furniture, flowers. If you have only a bottle of mineral water with your meal it is kept for you in a bucket of ice on your table and served as respectfully as though it were wine, and your humble half-bottle of non-vintage wine receives from the wine-waiter as respectful a treatment as though it were vintage. The bed linen is changed daily, and it is precisely that – linen; and to avoid creasing the fine linen the sheets are not tucked in at the sides but left hanging. In everything there is this exquisite attention to detail.

Whether it is all worth what it costs can only be a matter of opinion, though, in point of fact, except for the suites the prices of the rooms are very little if anything more than in other hotels on the Grand Canal; that is to say a room with a bath, overlooking the Canal, costs about £21 a night, per person. Personally if I were going to spend that much I would settle for the Gritti – and the elegance, and the *perfetto servizio* in which it specializes.

2

VENICE IN THE RAIN

ITALY is so associated with sunshine that it was surprising, to say the least, to arrive in Venice in the rain. It presented an entirely new aspect of the fabulous city. Something wild and strange and brooding. The low heavy clouds piled up over the Doges' Palace were not less than magnificent. When I had paid respects to the elegant gold-necked bottle in the bucket of ice next to the lovely carnations I went out, feeling a need to stretch my legs after some twenty-four hours on a train.

The Piazza San Marco is only round the corner from the Gritti, and it was pleasant to step out into the rainy coolness, and the dark, lowering sky was dramatic and exciting. I did not know, then, but was interested to learn later that Henry James regarded himself as fortunate – his word – to have seen Venice in the rain, 'all cold colour, and the steel-grey floor of the lagoon stroked the wrong way by the wind'. In sunshine Venice is all soft rose and faded gold and misty blue lagoon; that it could take on wildness seems, then, un-thinkable. But wild it was that evening, with dark clouds piled low over San Marco and the Doges' Palace, and the piazza flooded, with raised planks across, and the lagoon brimming over, and the moored launches jostling restlessly together, nudging each other, as though restrained against their will. There is the realization of the vulnerability of Venice, a memory of the tragedy of 1966 when the lagoon really did wash in, disastrously. Now, it seems, the Piazza San Marco is flooded because of the three days of continuous rain plus the autumn high tide. Some of the narrow lanes beside the small canals are impassable.

Despite the rain and the floodedness the San Marco area is milling with tourists strolling along under the arcades, gingerly crossing the planks across the square, drifting about in the Piazzetta – the 'ante-room' of the square proper – that which Napoleon declared was the finest open-air drawing-room in Europe. There was a preponderance of young people – which I had also noticed on the train – hairy, uni-sex as to clothing, amorous, walking with their arms about each other and pausing on and off to embrace. I used to think Paris was the city of young lovers, but I never saw so many kissing couples in Paris in the thirties as I saw in Venice some forty years on. Even in the damp, cold greyness of Venice after rain. I was told by the Chiari Sommariva young man who had met me at the railway station that the majority of tourists are American, though there were some English. No, he said, not many Germans. Germans do not come much to Venice. He should know, I suppose. I did, all the same, meet Germans.

On that first evening, as I lingered on the small bridge over the canal between the Doges' Palace and the old prison, spanned by the Bridge of Sighs, I was accosted by a young person of indeterminate sex who demanded of me, imperiously, in marked German accents, 'You speak English?' I admitted that I did. The creature then demanded, almost aggressively, 'The St Mark's Square – where is it?' That anyone standing by the Doges' Palace should inquire for St Mark's seemed to me most strange. 'It's here,' I said, confusedly, and waved in the direction of the piazzetta. The creature moved off without a word, accompanied by other uni-sex creatures with packs on their backs.

Across the brimming greyness of the lagoon the domes of the Santa Maria della Salute are dramatic against the piled-up masses of dark cloud. No mellow golden Canaletto painting this Venice, but Venice turbulent as its history.

It was not raining when I walked over to the Salute the following afternoon, across the Accademia bridge, but the sky was still heavy with dark, ominous-looking cloud, and the Piazza San Marco was still a lake. I crossed to the Salute to meet Miss Marion Cole, of the English end of the Venice in Peril Commitee. She had tele-

phoned me the evening before and we had agreed to meet at the
' 'bus stop' on the Salute side – the *vaporetti* station, that is to say –
and she would take me to the house of the Contessa Anna Maria
Ciogna, head of the preservation committee in Venice. I would meet
the contessa in the company of a Venice in Peril tourist group,
with whom the following day I was to make a tour of some of the
villas of the old Venetian aristocracy. The contessa regularly
receives these groups for discussion of the cause they all had at
heart. I had been interested in the Venice in Peril Committee since
the beautiful loan exhibition, *Venice Rediscovered*, at the Wilden-
stein Gallery at the end of 1972, organized in aid of the Venice in
Peril Fund, of which Lord Norwich is the chairman. I read the
articles of Sir Ashley Clarke, Vice-Chairman of the Fund, reprinted
from *The Ecologist* and elsewhere, available at the gallery and was
much impressed by the work of the British Committee. It was
therefore with a good deal of satisfaction that I learned that Miss
Cole and a VIP party would be in Venice when I was there and
that I was invited to meet them – and the contessa.

I arrived at the ' 'bus stop' a little early so took the opportunity to
go into the church of Santa Maria della Salute, built by Longhena
in the mid-seventeenth century in thanksgiving for the deliverance
of Venice from the plague. At the high altar there is a marble group
depicting the Virgin casting out the plague, and there are ceiling
paintings by Titian, but I thought as I had in 1964 when I had
visited this church that it was too grey and cold and grand. I
should perhaps give warning that I am not very good with the interiors of Italian churches; they all seem to me too vast, too full
of marble, museums rather than places of religious worship – which
is what, nowadays, they mostly are, anyhow.

When I emerged from the church and came down the wide sweep
of steps I found Miss Cole sheltering from the cold wind round a
corner. We had not previously met but knew each other intuitively.
She was as I had expected her to be, energetic, capable, elderly, with
a forthright, no-nonsense manner. The contessa's house was close
by and it was a relief to reach it and be admitted by a man-

servant into the small pleasant entrance hall out of the cold and grey.

We were escorted upstairs and the contessa awaited us in a charming drawing-room full of beautiful things. *She* was not at all as I had expected her to be; my imagination had somehow conjured up a figure of someone very old, stately, and eccentric; the woman who rose from a brocaded settee to greet us was slight and slim, very good-looking, very elegant; not young, but certainly not old. She has wonderful English, which she attributes, I understand, to having had an 'English nanny'. It would have been pleasant to have sat and talked with her in that beautiful L-shaped room, to have relaxed and talked informally, that is to say, but the matter in hand was Venice in Peril, and the group arrived from their Pensione alla Salute almost immediately, Seven women and three men, middle-aged – with the exception of one young woman I judged to be in her thirties – middle-class, serious-looking as be-fitted their serious purpose, and the occasion which for a brief moment before their arrival had seemed a social one became at once like a small committee meeting; the committee-meeting feeling was intensified by the fact that there were no introductions. They were just the current group, and this was 'the contessa', the meeting with whom was as much a part of their itinerary as their tour of the villas next day. But it was not entirely a 'committee meeting', for two white-jacketed, white-gloved menservants took up their positions beside a long table at one end of the room, and there were decanters and glasses, and plates and dishes of small eatables. Having had no lunch I averted my eyes; the goodies would be offered in due course; we were there to meet the contessa and discuss our common concern for Venice, and the refreshments, I reminded my hungry self, were only incidental.

For her part the contessa was entirely business-like, reseating herself on the settee whilst her guests disposed themselves about the room in a small half-circle, a tall, long-legged man balancing himself on a low pouffe in the middle (later I learned that he was one of the British Committee). The contessa did not so much address us as chair the debate; people asked questions, made suggestions, and our hostess held forth with a good deal of vehemence. It was evident that she had Venice written on her heart. The guests were a little shy, a little reserved, initially, in the English way, and to set the ball rolling I suggested that the flooding of St Mark's square by the rain of the last few days recalled the 1966 disaster. Could it happen again? But apparently it could not; that aspect of Venice in Peril was under control; there was now the barrage, protecting the lagoon from high tides and the exceptional inflow of water.*

The chief danger to Venice now was the pollution from the industrial areas on the mainland, one gathered – though, paradoxically, according to the contessa, more people came into Venice to work there last year than left it to work on the mainland .... I felt that I would have to work that one out. They came in as hotel staff to meet the seasonal demands of tourism, perhaps? For the contessa also complained that the local crafts are dying out because young people prefer to work in modern factories on the mainland, and also to live there, 'in cement boxes', in modern blocks rather then in decaying, crumbling Venice. Well, it is one thing, I thought, to live in a charming, well-preserved house in Venice, and quite another to live in one of those decaying and undoubtedly rat-ridden tenements on one of the less salubrious canals, in which there are no bathrooms, no 'mod cons' of any kind, and in some of them not even running water ... in that city saturated with water. I said something to this effect, but the contessa replied that the Italian government, under a new law, contributed up to seventy per cent of the cost of repairing old, decaying houses. I thought, but did

*In an article in *The Ecologist*, for March 1971, Sir Ashley Clarke explained that 'exceptionally high tides in the northern area of the Adriatic occur regularly at certain times of the year, of which early November is one. If at the same time the periodical oscillatory motion of the Adriatic (like the water in a bath) is piling up water in the neighbourhood of Venice, if the sea-currents are running in that direction, if there is a violent *scirocco* blowing and there is a storm in the mountains causing spate conditions in the rivers a formidable body of water is built up which is capable of crashing right over the present seaward defences.'

not think it polite to suggest, that many people in those decaying tenements would not be able to afford even thirty per cent of the cost of making their premises habitable. Eric Newby, writing in the *Observer* magazine for May 2, 1971, pointed out that most of the ills from which Venice suffers can be attributed to Marghera, an oil port, south of Mestre, which apart from the oil has innumerable factories, refineries and heavy industries, which pour their effluent into the lagoon. 'The last systematic analysis of its waters, in 1964,' he wrote, 'showed "cumulative pollution, slow and insidious which is now entering the category sub-acute".' He refers to Mestre as a 'vast sprawl of a place in which the majority of its workers live, in houses which although drab are at least dry', and which has been 'to some extent responsible for the progressive depopulation of the city'. He provides the very significant statistics that 'between 1852 and 1967 the population of Venice and the islands of Murano and Burano declined from 198,000 to 130,000', and that during the same period 'Mestre/Marghera doubled its population', and that the average age of the inhabitants of Venice is now about forty-eight. The young, in fact, go to the mainland as the contessa complained. But as Eric Newby pointed out, more than seventy per cent of the houses in Venice are without baths, and ninety per cent without central heating.

Venice is also sinking; not dramatically, nor even irretrievably; the subsidence is due to industry drawing off fresh water from under the bed of the lagoon, but the sinking of new wells in now forbidden. One of the contessa's guests suggested, hopefully, that perhaps Venice could be 'jacked up' like the temples at Abu Simbel in Egypt . . .

I think it was soon after this that the white-gloved young men standing so patiently by the long table at the other end of the room went into action, though there was a certain set-back when the contessa asked if anyone would like hot chocolate, and some people unfortunately did, which meant that those who didn't had to wait a little longer for the real stuff. Finally, however, white and red wine were served. By that time, anyhow, the 'meeting', as such, was at an end and the conversation had become general. The arrival of an attractive girl, introduced as 'Miss Cooper, Lord Norwich's daughter', broke up the party. We had anyhow been there two hours by then.

The group, with Miss Cole, walked back to their *pensione*, and I made my way, by the various lanes, to the Accademia bridge, with its lovely view down the Grand Canal to the church of Santa Maria della Salute, The plague it commemorates was in 1630, but the church was completed only in 1687, five years after Longhena's death.

Well, it had all been very interesting, at the contessa's, even if one was not entirely in accord with some of the things said, and I looked forward to getting to know some of the group better next day, on the tour of the villas. It would be the villas in the rain, by the look of the sky, still so heavy with dark cloud.

Venice so cold and grey; and up steps and down steps, crossing bridges when you come to them – no choice but to! – and some of the old houses looking ready to crumble into the canals. These old houses on the small canals are not palaces; many of them are not at all beautiful; but they are the *living* Venice, the homes of the greater part of the indigenous population, as opposed to Venice as the wonderful museum, the cultural storehouse of the Western world though how much longer this living Venice can stay alive, with such odds stacked against it, is debatable.

3
VILLAS AND VILLAGES

AT eight o'clock next morning a launch arrived to take me across the Grand Canal to the Pensione alla Salute. The morning was grey and cold and wet. At the Salute side the launch chugged into a narrow side-street of a canal and stopped at the steps up to the pavement in front of the *pensione*. It was by then eight-fifteen.

In the entrance lounge of the *pensione* there was a coming and going of people up and down the stairs behind the reception desk and a general to-ing and fro-ing. I inquired for Miss Cole and was told she was 'not down yet'. I seated myself at the side of the lounge and gradually realized that the people marching up and down the stairs, and crossing and re-crossing the lounge, and peering out anxiously through the glass panes of the door on to the canal, were the people with whom I had been yesterday at the contessa's. I became aware, too, of a certain agitation.

A woman I recognized from yesterday seated herself next to me. I remarked, conversationally, that it was not a very good day for touring the villas, and she replied that some people were in two minds about going; there had been a lot of discussion at breakfast, she said. I expressed surprise, for, surely, I suggested, we wouldn't be much exposed to the weather, only getting in and out of the coach, and other than that we'd be under cover. She declared that *she* intended going, anyway, and it was clear from her well-water-proofed attire, from head to toe, that the weather would not present any problem for her. Indeed, she looked almost ready for an ascent of Everest. She seemed amused by the restless to-ings and fro-ings and peerings out of the others, watching with a small ironic smile. The scene had, in fact, a certain comic element, with the continual movement to the front door and anxious peering, and some people

reporting, hopefully, that it wasn't raining much, only to be immediately countered by those who insisted that it was raining hard. One
woman declared, emphatically, that her husband wasn't going, and
was still having breakfast. It was the voice of Doom.

In the midst of the fussation the door opened and a tall, heavily-
built, elderly man wearing a raincoat and beret came in out of the
rain. He nodded to the company in general, stated, 'I am the guide,'
then seated himself, took some documents out of an inner pocket
and became immersed in them. His presence added to the acuteness of
the question – to go, or not to go ? In view of the weather, and some
people dropping out, would the tour still be on ? There was, too, a
somewhat querulous demand for Miss Cole; why wasn't she there to
advise them? – they didn't actually say in their hour of need, but
that was the implication.

At eight-thirty Miss Cole descended into the lounge, serenely. We
exchanged greetings and I told her, 'There's a great flap as to whether
the tour is on or not, with all this rain. Some people seem inclined not
to go. They want your advice.' I added that I didn't understand the
flap because what was all the fuss about? Those who were prepared to brave the weather would go, and those who weren't could
remain behind.

Miss Cole explained that it wasn't as simple as that; the tour could
only be done as a *group* – there had to be a minimum of ten people.
It was a rule of the agency with whom it had been arranged. So,
obviously, if people fell out if wouldn't be on. It would be bad luck
on the people who wanted to go, but that was the way it was.

People closed in on her, and she dealt with their protests and
questions with admirable unflappability. I don't know, really, what
happened, but there came a point at which we all trooped out into
the rain and trudged along beside the murky little canal, following
the portly figure of the guide, who after a few yards paused to
count us – but we were eleven, for full measure.

We were to walk to the Accademia *vaporetto* stop, it seemed, not
the Salute, which was a little nearer. A woman stumping along beside me observed, bitterly, when the guide announced this, that it

was 'just that much further to walk in the rain'. She had been one of those who had wanted to call the whole thing off.

I learned, later, that my arrival by launch had falsely raised everyone's hopes; they had believed that the launch had come to take them to the Piazzale Roma and the coach – that it had been laid on because of the bad weather. It had been a blow when the launch had chugged off back to its 'taxi rank' on the Grand Canal.

It was the rush-hour and the *vaporetto* was packed, with standing-room-only when we boarded it – and barely standing room at that. For some of the group, unaccustomed to the rigours of public transport, it must have been a horror; for others of us it was just a 'bus in the rush-hour, unpleasant, but an inescapable fact of life.

When the group had extricated itself from the *vaporetto* and reassembled at the Piazzale Roma the guide counted his flock again, then led us to the waiting coach. His flock were a glum-looking lot, but I got the feeling that for him so long as they were all present-and-correct it was all that mattered.

Aboard the coach wet head-coverings were removed and shaken, dripping mackintoshes hung on the backs of unused seats; everyone was damp and disgruntled. Certain phrases recurred in the grumbling: 'bad management', and 'no proper arrangements'.

Yet the weather was nobody's fault, and the memorandum regarding the tour stated clearly that departure from the *pensione* to the Piazzale Roma, for the coach, would be by 'public launch'. To me it all seemed a much ado about nothing very much; the weather was unfortunate, but we hadn't had to walk very far in the rain; the *vaporetto* was uncomfortably crowded, but it was a journey of only a few minutes, and we were all under cover; and now, with a whole coach to ourselves, we had plenty of room in which to spread our wet things. It seemed a pity to spread the grievances too.

(Later I was bound to admit that the group had a grievance or two – beginning with the fact that only one of the villas on the itinerary was open, and that at that one we spent far too long. My own feeling was one of relief that only one of the villas was open – that it would have been tedious trooping in and out of the coach

Venice, the Rialto bridge: 'there is a very fine view along the Grand Canal from the Ponte Rialto, with palaces on either hand.'

The Piazza San Marco: 'the mosaic façade of St Mark's has to be approached across the square for the full impact of its splendour.'

Venice, from the Accademia bridge: 'a lovely view down the Grand Canal to the church of Santa Maria della Salute.'

The Doges' Palace: 'warm and rosy in the evening light.'

in the rain to view half a dozen interiors; apart from the fact that
I was a guest and pleased with whatever offered. Had I paid good
money for the tour I might very well have shared the disgruntlement.)

Anyhow, we hurtled out of Venice across the lagoon in the
direction of Mestre, passing the huge chemical works which em-
ploys seven thousand people, the guide told us, and which contributes so much to the pollution from which Venice suffers, and
turning westward were soon on the 'villa route', with the narrow
river Brenta on our left, and villas galore, left and right. The
coach slows down for the guide to point out a fifteenth-century
villa beside the canalized river that goes on to Venice; there are
weeping willows and there is a pillared portico. 'Palladian,' says the
guide, and we gaze respectfully. Certainly it is a handsome house.

All these villas at either side of the Brenta were designed as summer homes, retreats from the heat of the city, though it can surely
not have been much less hot on the mainland then in the lagoon;
still, it was 'the country', and life in the villa was different from that
in the *palazzo*; for one thing the villa was always set in a garden,
with trees and fountains. The banks of the Brenta were popular
because of the accessibility by boat to and from both Venice and
Padua. In the old days a large barge, called a *burchiello*, plied
between the two cities, and Hugh Honour, in his admirable *Companion Guide to Venice* (1965), says that there was a seventeenth-
century proverb to the effect that the barge would sink the day it
did not have on board a friar, a student, and a courtesan, and that
Goethe recorded how much he enjoyed a voyage in it. The *burchiello*
has been revived in modern, motorized form, complete with a bar
and a multilingual hostess who provides the commentary. The
9,500 lire fare (1974) includes luncheon at Oriago, local guides,
entrance fees to the villas. The return journey is made by public
bus from Padua. The *burchiello* plies from Venice mid-June to mid-
September, on Mondays, Wednesdays and Saturdays, and on alter-
nate days from Padua to Venice. It would seem to be a comfort-
able and pleasant way of making the villas tour.

C

But either way, by boat or coach, you come soon to the Villa Foscari, more popularly known as the Villa della Malcontenta, so called, it is said, because one of the Foscari ladies was 'imprisoned' there – banished by her family, or, some say, by her husband tired of her cantankerousness. It was designed by Andrea Palladio and built about 1560. We peer at it though the rain-misted windows of the coach; it looks handsome enough, set back amongst trees.

There are innumerable villas after that, large and small, mostly fifteenth and sixteenth century, but a few as late as the eighteenth, and you pass through a long, straggling village with an open-air market of fruit, flowers, vegetables, and the canalized river is 'very nice in the evening, coming from Padua', says the guide, 'with a beautiful light on the water'. We pass through a shoe-manufacturing centre, not beautiful, but 'giving work to many villages in the district', and one recalls, then, the beautiful Italian shoes. There are, as might be expected, a great many new houses in this area, but no ugly blocks of flats, and soon there are trees in a main street, and an old church with a brightly painted mural above the porch.

We come to Dolo, where there are many fine villas, and which is the background for Aldous Huxley's story *Little Mexican*, published in 1924, and which I re-read before setting out on this Italian journey, and looked at again on my return with an even greater appreciation. As a story it doesn't really amount to much, but as a description of the villas on the Brenta it is superb. 'The Brenta, sunk deep between the banks of its canal', and 'to right and left, on either bank of the river . . . a glimpse of some enchanting mansion, gay and brilliant even in decay'. The narrator of the story reflects that it was in these villas that Casanova used to come and spend the summers, 'seducing the chamber-maids, taking advantage of terrified marchionesses in *caleches* during thunder-storms, bamboozling soft-witted old senators in Venice with his fortune-telling and black magic. Gorgeous and happy scoundrel!'

After an area of vineyards we reach the small town of Stra, and the Villa Nazionale, or Pisani, though it is more strictly the *Palazzo*

Pisani, for it is huge – the largest of all the country houses on the Brenta.

We alighted from the coach. It was still raining – hard.

The Villa Pisani was built in the eighteenth century and is only one of the several country houses of the Pisani family. Its front façade is yellow and covered with virginia creeper – 'like an English house,' says the guide. It does not, however, look at all English to me. Hugh Honour says that it always reminds him of 'the villa of Senator Pococurante, the prototype of the dissatisfied millionaire visited by Candide'.

The entrance hall is massive with pillars; there is an inner court-yard, and a view of the garden, which is really a park. In this im-posing garden a canal leads to a handsome yellow mansion with a portico, and statuary on the roof – and it is startling to learn that this was the stables! There are trees and walls and statuary, and the guide tells us that there is a 'labyrinth' – a maze – and a priest's house. It is all quite fabulous, and it would have been fascinating to walk in this best-preserved-garden of the Brenta villas, but the rain prevented.

Hugh Honour says that many famous people have stayed at the Villa Pisani – 'Napoleon, Eugène Beauharnais (while Viceroy of Italy), a Czar of Russia and an Emperor of Austria'. He adds that 'unfortunately in 1934 it also witnessed one event of tragic consequence – the first meeting between Mussolini and Hitler'.

We leave the inner courtyard, with the massive yellow pillars and the faded red murals, and mount the wide staircase, and there begins a seemingly endless procession of vast rooms, with painted ceilings and elaborately decorated walls. When he discovers that we are English the guide indicates Queen Anne chairs, for our satisfaction – and in vindication of his own knowledgeability (and he is, in fact, remarkably knowledgeable).

There are Venetian glass chandeliers, and a series of painted rooms – ante-chambers – and a chapel with an altar brought from San Gimignano, and a marble statue of the Madonna and Child with gilt crowns. There is a 'Room of the Doges', full of medallions of the doges on the walls; there is a room full of Longhi prints, and a room with a huge wall painting by Simoni, which the guide explains, pointing with his still damp umbrella; there is a room full of flower prints... impossible to catalogue it all, and saturation point is soon reached. The rooms lead out of one another, as Hugh Honour says, 'in a seemingly endless sequence', but there is one room, the ballroom, for which alone it would be worth going to Stra, as he says, for there is a Tiepolo ceiling of the Pisani family in glory – *Gloria della casa Pisani*. It is so grandiose it is quite fantastic. I had thought it was the Pisani family ascending into heaven, but Hugh Honour explains it as depicting the glory of the Pisani family, trumpeted by an angel to the four corners of the earth. Upon which one can only comment, Well, I never! It is anyhow Very Impressive; and must have been very exhausting to paint. It was it seems, Tiepolo's last work in Italy, finished early in 1762, before, says Hugh Honour, 'he set off on his journey to Spain where disillusion and death awaited him'.

According to my notes there comes a point at which I wilt, feeling that I cannot look or listen any more, 'and it is cold in the huge empty rooms' – which seem to go on forever. The 'sparseness', according to Hugh Honour, is 'historically correct; houses contained far less furniture in the eighteenth century than they do today'.

It goes on; there is a white and gold bedroom in which Napoleon 'slept only one night'. There is a portrait of him in the room. There is a room with a white and gold sedan chair, with the arms of Austria, the eagle with two heads, the chair designed 'to carry the empress of Austria'. There is a billiards room; and a room with more wall paintings by Simoni, battle scenes. There is a banqueting hall with huge chandeliers and a fresco after Tiepolo ...

But we are out at last, and on the canal there is a boat going to Padua ... for which we, also, are bound.

Padua is a city of which I would like to know more; much more. I have been in and out of it three times, but each time with less than an hour there. It is one of the oldest and most interesting cities in Italy. As we drove in from Stra the arcaded streets of the old town reminded me of Baghdad. The narrow streets were choked with cars, and overlooking the gardens which contain the remains of a Roman amphitheatre, and the Scrovegni chapel, with the Giotto frescoes, rises a most monstrous skyscraper tower. At the Scrovegni chapel disgruntlement again raises it head – that we should have only twenty minutes here, after an hour-and-a-half at that boring Villa Pisani. . . . But in fact twenty minutes is enough, for the chapel is swarming with school-children, chewing gum and sucking sweets and paying precious little attention to the frescoes, but milling about and making it impossible for anyone else to view them properly. Under such circumstances twenty minutes is ample; to examine the frescoes properly hours are needed, and an empty chapel. On the altar there are statues of the Madonna and Child by Giovanni Pisano. It is interesting that the chapel was built by Enrico Scrovegni at the beginning of the fourteenth century in expiation of his father's usury, and as a plea for the Virgin's inter-cession on his behalf. Thus though the frescoes depict the traditonal scenes from the life of Christ the sin of usury is stressed. The guide insisted on the revolutionary aspect of these frescoes, the break-away from the traditionalism of the Byzantine. Hugh Honour says that 'in the Scrovegni chapel one is, indeed, present at the birth of modern painting in Europe', though it took Venetian artists one hundred and fifty years to catch up.

With the swarms of children milling around it was not possible to take in much on that occasion, but there was the impact of some-thing profoundly human and dramatic, and of strong reds and blues, and the familiar New Testament scenes powerfully presented. I did not know, then, that I would have an opportunity to revisit the chapel under more congenial conditions, and left at the end of the twenty minutes with a despairing feeling of frustration. On the next occasion there was more time, and the chapel was almost empty, and it was possible to feel something of the immense power – and the glory – of this astonishing work. Dante came to Padua from

Bologna in 1306 and was Giotto's guest, and it is generally accepted that Giotto began his work in the chapel in that year, under Dante's influence.

By the time we reached the attractive small mountainy town of Bassano del Grappa, with its fifteenth-century walls, its covered wooden bridge across the Brenta, its castle and its vineyards, we had two fairly urgent requirements, both uninhibitedly admitted by both sexes: we needed what the females, anyhow, referred to as 'the loo', and we needed alcohol; in that order. We made these requirements known to the guide when we arrived at the small hotel at which were to lunch, making it clear that they took precedence over eating. Also that our need was great. He was entirely sympathetic and waved us off, male and female, in the appropriate directions.

When we reassembled, relieved and relaxed, the second requirement asserted itself even more strongly. Each child now needed *a drink*. Not for thirst-quenching purposes but from frail human need. We had been through *a lot* since we left the *pensione* in Venice more than four hours ago. Our nervous condition needed the boost of alcohol. There was not an abstainer amongst us. We wanted strong drink; and we wanted it quick.

But this was something the guide did not understand as clearly as he had understood our more primitive need. Yes, yes, when we ordered the lunch there would be wine. A Scottish university professor told him, sternly, that we were not talking about wine with our meal; we were talking about *drinks*, *before* the meal. *Where was the bar?* It was a fair question, and in fact the bar was close beside the entrance to the lounge, but it had a derelict appearance and nobody was manning it. The guide, helplessly, waved us to the restaurant, which was a covered verandah, very pleasant. The waiter, he said, we would speak with the waiter. The waiter was very pleased by our entry into the restaurant, and approached with pad and pencil at the ready to take our orders for *tagliatelli*, *vitello*, and the rest of it.

Our friend from Edinburgh University stated with good Scottish precision and firmness that before we ordered *food* we needed *drinks* – sherry, vermouth, Campari . . . I think *Campari* was the key word that unlocked understanding; Campari, a drink taken before a meal. I ordered a Campari-soda, and when the waiter came round again to take our orders for food I ordered another. That anyone would want to order sherry in Italy puzzled me, but sherry was ordered and obtained, and food was ordered, and wine, and the group began to relax. The difficult part, after all, was behind us; we had 'done' the villas, after a fashion, and the rain had ceased and the sun come out, and Bassano seemed an attractive place, and wasn't it famous for some kind of fiery spirit called *grappa*? Well, it is, and later we were to sample it, but right now we had to deal with *tagliatelli*, which I dislike, disliking Italian food in general – all that *pasta*! – and *vitello*, which is veal, which I never eat, and never have eaten, on principle; that didn't leave anything but some very underdone beef, accompanied by some very garlicky sauté potatoes, so one way and another not my kind of a meal, but there was a sweet of ice-cream and cake, which was delicious, followed by some *caffè espresso* which was very nasty.

People valiantly ordered wine with the meal; valiantly because when they had had their drinks I don't think any of them particularly wanted the harsh red or white wines that were – namelessly – offered. They ordered them, I think, to show willing; as the English do. The wine came in red and yellow plastic decanters designed as fishes – large fish for the full bottles, small fish for the half-bottles, lurid yellow for the white wine, lurid scarlet for the red; very nasty. I was glad to be sticking to Campari-soda, which at least came in a glass.

But the drinks, and the wine in the dreadful plastic fishes, at least produced euphoria, and according to my notes 'we all felt a lot less jaded when we returned to the coach'.

We drove on through the pleasant mountainy landscape to Possagno, the birthplace of the sculptor, Antonio Canova. He is buried in the Doric Pantheon on the hillside above the village, the 'temple of Canova', designed by him as the village church. It is a fantastic place, inside and out, all fluted columns without and white and gold and marble splendour within – 'effective as a decoration', as a man in our party observed, drily, 'but no religious atmosphere'. But a German woman in the party was quite cross about it; she didn't think it beautiful, but merely pretentious and vulgar, I thought it beautiful, in its cold, classical fashion, but was only so astonished at the idea of it as a village church.

We come to Asolo: another lovely mountainy place, presented by Venice to Queen Catherine Cornaro, in exchange for Cyprus. Her castle is perched on the hilltop above the little town, and in the little museum there are memorials of her and of Robert Browning, who loved the place and used it for the scene of *Pippa Passes*. His son, and Eleonora Duse, are buried there, in the cemetery of Sant' Anna. Monte Grappa rises behind, and there is a deep valley terraced with vineyards. There are narrow arcaded streets, and old houses with faded murals. There is a church with a gold medallion of the Madonna above the porch, and inside a painting by Lorenzo Lotto of the Assumption. It is a remarkably grand church for so small a place.

It was very pleasant mooching about in that curiously Austrian-Tirol little town in the warm sunshine. The guide led us up a steep cobbled street to a café with a garden and terrace overlooking the valley, and there was a pomegranate tree hung with fruit, and a splendid view of Monte Grappa across the Venetian plain. At the café we tasted *grappa*, a fiery spirit, made from the mush after the wine has been extracted, we were told. I thought it tasted like Calvados, only nastier. We anyhow gulped it down, on the principle of when in Asolo do as the Asolos do, and the guide told us that one of Catherine Cornaro's courtiers had invented the word *asolare*, meaning to sit in the sun and relax – amuse oneself. Robert Browning entitled his last book of poems, *Asolando*, 'for love of the place'. We are shown the very narrow arcaded street known as 'Robert Browning's street', and the 'house of Robert Browning', which is four-square and covered with virginia creeper.* There are the hills of Padua in the distance, and it is nice that the guide calls them *eels*.

We return to the coach and soon there is another villa – the Villa Barbaro, at Maser; it is long and low and yellow, very handsome, set off by the tall dark cypresses behind it. It was built by Palladio, for Daniel Barbaro, the patriarch of Aquileia, and contains frescoes by Veronese – Hugh Honour says that the main rooms are 'masterpieces of Paolo Veronese . . . in his unique combination of coolness and splendour', and that the same qualities mark the statue-guarded nymphaeum behind the house, 'which realizes a Renaissance dream of classical tranquillity'. The villa is open to the public on Tuesdays, Fridays, and the first Sunday in the month; unfortunately we were there on a Thursday. The chapel of the villa is also the work of Palladio, with a white interior 'of crystalline perfection'. From the coach it was only possible to note that it was circular and beautiful, harmonizing with the villa, and that there were murals at each side of the entrance.

There was a final villa at Zerman, the Villa Condulmer, set in lovely gardens, and here, according to the itinerary, tea was to be taken; but it was by then already six o'clock and a wedding party had arrived at the villa and no one was disposed to cope with this coach party and tea. I personally did not mind not having tea; so far as I was concerned it was too late and going on for what a friend of mine calls 'drinky time', but the group were again put out, all the good humour engendered by Bassano and Asolo evaporating, and it was a disgruntled party that left the coach at the Piazzale Roma and was shepherded to a crowded *vaporetto* to be ferried

* In fact the house belonged to his friend, Mrs Arthur Bronson, to whom he dedicated the *Asolanda* poems which were published on December 12, 1889, the day on which he died in Venice, at the Palazzo Rezzonico, which his son had bought. In the dedicatory letter to Mrs Bronson, written on October 15, at Asolo, Browning refers to the palace 'tower' of Queen Catherine Cornaro overlooking the house, which was called La Mura. Mrs Bronson was a wealthy American woman, with some small literary ability. She also had a house on the Grand Canal, the Casa Alvisi, at which Browning also stayed.

back to the Salute side of the Grand Canal. 'Bassano and Asolo were nice,' I urged; they agreed, but complained that from first to last the villas had been closed, except for that boring great place at Stra, which wasn't really a villa at all, but a palace, and if we hadn't spent so long there we'd have arrived at the Villa Condulmer in time for tea. . . .

It was true enough, and it was a pity about the Villa Barbaro (now known as the Villa Volpi) and its lovely chapel, but it had been a long day and I was tired and all I wanted to do was to walk back over the Accademia Bridge to the Gritti and lie flat. Not *talk* any more.

4

THE LIDO AND CHIOGGIA

'TRY to see Chioggia,' I had been urged, before I set out, 'attractive old town and Italy's chief fishing port. Nice trip in the lagoon.' I was entirely willing to; I like fishing ports – Cornwall, Britanny, anywhere. After the ten-hour villas stint a nice-trip-in-the-lagoon next day seemed just the thing. I consulted the Blue Guide. 'From Venice to Chioggia: motor-vessel in two hours from the Riva degli Schiavoni, an interesting voyage through the Isole del Dolore in the s. half of the lagoon.' It doesn't say so in the Blue Guide but I had been told that there was a steamer at 11.34 a.m.

There was, too. I made my way to San Marco in pale sunshine that burnished the wonderful gold mosaics of the façade of that fantastic Byzantine dream of a cathedral, and past the Doges' Palace, warm and rosy again, and along the waterfront to the little bridge over the canal from which you view the Bridge of Sighs, and on along to the wider waterfront of the degli Schiavoni, and there in front of the Hotel Danieli was a notice board about *vaporetti* departures, and sure enough there was one at 11.34 and Chioggia was writ plain.

'Chioggia *ritorno*,' I said, equally plainly, at the booking office. I don't know if that is correct Italian, but it had to do. The clerk who issued the ticket said something about the Lido, but this I assumed to mean change-at-the-Lido, or via-the-Lido, and that arrived there all would be revealed.

On the boat a man seated in front of me, by dint of glancing repeatedly over his shoulder, sketched the young woman at my side – a fact of which she was obviously disapprovingly aware, frowning, and continually averting her head. This, however, did not deter the man with the sketching pad and charcoal; he worked with rapid strokes, and the result, achieved in a few minutes, was, it has to be said, a remarkably good likeness. With a small, hopeful smile he handed the sketch over his shoulder to the young woman's male companion – her husband, I thought. The man glanced at it, smiled, and said something to the young woman, but she turned away, impatiently, disdainfully. The artist continued to smile – hopefully. The man brought out his wallet. '*Mille lire*,' the artist murmured. The man passed over a thousand lire note. The artist murmured his *grazie*, then, with a polite gesture, took the sketch from the other man, neatly rolled it, fastened it with an elastic band, and handed it back, smiling, with a slight inclination of his head. The courteous transaction was complete. The artist then sat with his back four-square to those behind him for the rest of the journey. The young woman maintained her contemptuous lack of interest, not speaking to her companion, who sat smiling, a little sheepishly, until the smile finally died of inanition.

Well, I thought, as we chugged across the blue water of the lagoon, it was one way of earning a living. The sort of thing 'Corvo' might have done. (He stooped, in fact, to things a good deal lower in his Venetian struggle for survival.) A few trips to and from the Lido for a small fare, and a few sketches at a thousand lire a time... Occasionally, I suppose, he would draw a blank (with some adamant foreigner – that couple were Italian) but more often than not, his prices being low and his likenesses good, he would effect a sale. It was all very impertinent, of course, sketching people without their permission, embarrassing them, and then expecting them to buy the end-product. But as the Americans say, 'You gotta live!'

At the Lido the *vaporetto* emptied. I inquired for Chioggia and was astonished to receive the word *autobus* in reply. I wandered away and crossed the road and turned into a wide tree-lined boulevard, and coming to a 'bus stop inquired of two young men standing at it for Chioggia. They understood 'Chioggia' and I understood that the 'bus stop for it was at the other side of the road. I crossed the road and stood at the 'bus stop; and stood; and stood. The fact that nobody else was waiting was discouraging. I began not to believe in Chioggia. There were various road-signs, but none said Chioggia, Then I noticed one that said Tourist Office. At the Tourist Office they would know the times that 'buses departed – if at all – for Chioggia.

I found the office and learned that there was no 'bus until one o'clock. That, anyhow, gave me an hour in which to explore the Lido a little, and I set off down the tree-lined boulevard, the Gran Viale Santa Maria Elisabetta, with its shops and patisseries and café-terraces and restaurants, and at the end of it came to the open sea. There were public gardens and big hotels, and a sandy beach, scruffy, with kiosks and snack bars and coarse grass and litter; but also white waves curling in from the Adriatic – the real sea. There were only a few people about; it was out-of-season for the Lido. Adjoining this unattractive beach there was another one, with beehived-shaped bathing huts, but it was sealed off – all the beaches at the Lido, save two, this scruffy one and one at the other end, are private, belonging to the big hotels, villas, bathing establishments. I was half minded to go and look at the huge old Excelsior Palace Hotel, a relic of the twenties, and at the Grand-Hôtel des Bains, which was used in the making of that deplorable film of Thomas Mann's fine novella, *Death in Venice*, but did not feel I had sufficient time if I was to get that one o'clock 'bus to Chioggia, so turned my back on the sea and retraced my steps up the boulevard Elisabetta.

The 'bus had arrived when I got back and a number of people had boarded it. Having procured a map at the Tourist Office I knew that the 'bus would traverse the length of the sandbar, but was puzzled as to how it would get to Chioggia, since some water was involved. Was there, perhaps, a bridge?

There was no bridge. At the end of a long and dull 'bus ride we all disembarked, and what there was was a ferry. In my innocence – and in spite of the map – I had thought the ferry would take us to Chioggia, and was astonished that when we alighted from the ferry there was another 'bus – to a place called Pellestrina, and then, fantastically, another ferry. But when we alighted from that second ferry it really was Chioggia. In my notes I recorded: Pellestrina is the frowsy place beyond rubbish dumps and a walled graveyard. But according to the Blue Guide, Pellestrina, 'strung out along its narrow sandbar, is a fishing village with a lace industry'. There is also strung out along the sandbar a breakwater called the Murazzi, built in the mid-eighteenth century to control the force of the Adriatic.

We reached the Porto di Chioggia, at about two o'clock, and the thought of the ferry and 'bus, and ferry and 'bus, back was oppressive. I noted with satisfaction that there was a boat back soon after three.

There are souvenir kiosks near the pier, and stalls offering shells for sale; there is a small, humped stone bridge over a canal; there are tall, narrow old houses, and there is a smell of the sea. Across the bridge you come to the broad main street, cobbled, its pavements on a level with the road and so crowded with café-terraces that it is necessary to walk in the road, where young people charge about in all directions on scooters. There are also numerous cars. Off this noisy main street, the Corso del Popolo, there are dark arcades with small shops, and narrow side-streets with washing suspended from side to side. There are baroque churches; there is a town hall, and a campanile. The afternoon was warm, and I trudged up one side of the Corso del Popolo and down the other, over the cobbles, always in imminent danger of being mown down by a car or scooter, and was glad to get back to the Ponte Vigo, and the Piazzetta, with its column supporting the Lion of St Mark, and the reassuring sight of the waiting steamer.

The return journey was less tedious, for the 'bus stayed on the ferry from Pellestrina. Chioggia is 'picturesque', I suppose, from the water, like the islands of the lagoon, but there is nothing much behind that picturesque façade of old houses, and it was with satisfaction that I read in Hugh Honour's guide that though Chioggia is 'one of the most important Italian fishing ports, its fleet ranging the whole of the Adriatic, it is of a run-down appearance, and the poverty of its streets is emphasized by the rigid grid plan which conceals nothing'.

That I did not go into the churches might be in retrospect a matter for regret, but that Hugh Honour dismisses them as 'containing a multitude of paintings and statues by minor Venetian masters, mostly of the eighteenth century'. It seems only right to record, however, that in the baroque church by the bridge, San Domenico, there is a painting of St Paul by Carpaccio (1520), and a painting of Christ crucified, conversing with saints, ascribed to Tintoretto. Also that there is an early fourteenth-century building on the Corso del Popolo which is now a market-hall. There is also a cathedral, the interior reconstructed by Longhena, after a fire in 1623, 'notable for its rich marble decoration'.

James Morris, in his splendid book, *Venice* (1960), writes of 'the musty churches of Chioggia . . . hung with the votive offerings of fishermen', and of the 'stumpy winged lion' on the pillar near the quay as a joke among Venetians, who call it, he says, the Cat of St Mark's. 'A streak of pathos,' he writes, 'an echo of ridicule, seems to infuse the life of this ancient fishing town, which still feels palsied, scabrous and tumble-down', but in spite of this sense of degeneracy its fishing catches travel each day 'in refrigerated trucks as far as Milan, Rome and Innsbruck'. But the 'rabble of touts, car park men, beggar boys and assorted obsequious attendants' on the quayside I did not see; nor the black-shawled fishermen's wives on the quayside 'doing obviously traditional things with needles, pieces of wood, nets and pestles'. That was thirteen years ago; when I stepped ashore at Chioggia, in September, 1973, there was no one much on the quayside, only the sellers of souvenirs and postcards and shells and dried sea-horses, and very few tourists wandered around.

And I am sure it is a 'nice trip in the lagoon' – when the boats are running.

5

SERENATA ON THE GRAND CANAL

As the distinguished American writer, Mary McCarthy, points out in her famous little book, *Venice Observed* (1956), Venice is hard on the rational mind; the rational instinct is to put up a resistance to 'this grossly advertised wonder . . . this painted deception, this cliché'. Ruskin came to detest it, and busied himself exposing its cultural frauds; Henry James, though he remained a faithful lover, complained that it had become 'a vast museum', where there was 'nothing left to discover or describe', and where 'originality of attitude is utterly impossible'. That, as we say nowadays, is very true. Venice has been living off tourism for centuries, and will continue to do so until it finally sinks into the lagoon – if it does – and to people who assert that it could be made into a 'live city' in its own right I retort with a terse five-lettered word. As Mary McCarthy says, it is no use pretending that tourist Venice is not the real Venice, it *is* – 'the gondolas, the sunsets, the changing lights . . . the pigeons, the glass beads, the *vaporetto*. Venice is a folding picture-post-card of itself.'

Take it or leave it, that's the way it is; and I am perfectly happy to take it. Venice is unique; it is the world's most beautiful city, and the world's most wonderful museum. I am profoundly grateful that it exists, and blessed are mine eyes. The tourists from all over the world, milling in the Piazza San Marco, cannot make the face of the basilica less than fabulous, a miracle of rare device, something truly out of this world. Nothing can detract from it, because it is *there*; beyond all telling in its beauty; and inviolate.

So you accept it or you don't, and if you don't you are the poorer.

The Church of Santa Maria della Salute: 'built in the mid-seventeenth century in thanksgiving for the delivery of Venice from the plague.'

The Gritti Palace: 'built for Andrea Gritti, the 67th Doge of Venice (1455–1538), and now one of the most beautiful hotels in Europe.'

Florence, the Ponte Vecchio: 'with its little shops, and now a pedestrian thoroughfare.' The oldest bridge in Florence.

The Ponte di Santa Trinità: opened in 1957; an exact replica of the bridge of 1569.

I am of those who accept it, happily, gratefully – the triteness, the cliché, the romance, the potency of its spells.

I have, therefore, no inhibitions at all about admitting that I found a night *serenata* on the Grand Canal romantic and moving, even though I realized that it was a tourist thing, and despite the fact that James Morris refers to it in his book as 'that ghastly serenade' – whilst acknowledging that the Venetians themselves lean tenderly from their balconies, 'to hear the music, and watch the undeniably romantic bobbing of the gondola prows in the half-light'. I opened the hotel window and leaned out – like the Venetians – and on the shadowy water below there drifted past a flotilla of gondolas, like great dark swans. In the middle of the flotilla there was a special carnival gondola, with a super-structure amidships, strung with fairy lights, and from this floating stage came the voice of a singer, a woman's voice, strong, vibrant, passionate. The form of the singer could be made out, indistinct, but feminine, as the flotilla drifted past. Not knowing Italian I do not know of what she sang, but it can hardly be other than of love and longing . . . I have heard such yearning songs amongst the Arabs. Perhaps it brought out the sentimental worst in me, but I found it romantic.

When the song ended there was a vigorous round of applause. The woman singer was followed by a man, whose style was 'operatic', full of tremolos; he bellowed forth – there was no poignancy, and the applause was merely polite.

From the rear of the flotilla came the sound of an accordion, which had its own kind of *café-chantant* romanticism.

When the *serenata* had passed I closed the window and lay on my bed wondering about it all – what it meant in hard cash to the gondoliers, their living undermined by motor-boats; and what it meant to the people in the gondolas – people from Miami and Manchester and London, and all over. Buying an illusion of romance at four thousand lire a time in the Grand Canal, and cheap at the price, you might say, in a harshly materialistic world. 'An illusion of romance' – but what is romance? The beautiful and poetic re-

D

moved from everyday life? The definition might serve – since medieval chivalry no longer comes into it. To drift in a flotilla of gondolas along the Grand Canal, at night, whilst a woman with a strong, sweet voice sings songs of love and longing, the vibrant voice carrying powerfully over the shadowy water – yes, that could be defined as romantic.

Mary McCarthy speaks of the absence of passion in the Venetian temperament as contributing to the unreal character of Venetian life, and says that in the 'traditional Venetian serenades, played from cruising gondolas, the songs are all Neapolitan'. Which accounts, no doubt, for the heavy vibrato of the male singer in that *serenata* I watched and listened to from the window in the Gritti Palace.

I thought about the gondoliers who are so much a feature of the Venetian scene, but whose calling is as imperilled as Venice itself. All the chroniclers of Venice insist on the imperishability of the gondola, and therefore by implication of the gondolier, in Venetian life, but it is difficult to see how the gondola can survive against the *vaporetto* and the motor-launch, any more than the horse-drawn cab sould survive against the taxi. The gondola can only survive, if at all, as a tourist luxury – an expensive relic of the past for those who can afford it. It is difficut to imagine Venice without gondolas, but, as Hugh Honour says, 'despite the patronage of summer visitors the gondola is dying' – the charges are too high for general purposes, and 'to get from one place to another, most visitors – like the Venetians – either walk or use the public boat services'. The gondola is beautiful, with its decorated prow, its little brass sea-horses at either side of the two seats, and in its gracefulness, and it is traditionally romantic, associated with romantic love. 'Its very name has the ring of amorous poetry', Hugh Honour declares, and cites Alfred de Musset as saying that no one who has not been in a gondola by moonlight has explored all the mysteries of love. All the same, when he and George Sand arrived in Venice, after dark, the gondola which was their transport to the Hotel Danieli 'looked like a coffin', André Maurois reminds us,*

* In *Lélia, the Life of George Sand*. English Edition, 1953

and it was that same evening in the hotel that de Musset told his mistress that he did not love her. He took to drinking in the Venetian slums, and to the embraces of the dancing girls of the Fenice theatre. In the end he fell ill, which brought the young Italian doctor, Pagello, into George's life, and she became his mistress. The gondola had indeed proved to be a coffin. George Sand made a number of notes for Venetian stories, and eventually returned to Paris, having absorbed all that Venice could give her – of love, and 'copy'.

Mark Twain was another for whom the gondola was funereal. 'We reached Venice at eight in the evening,' he wrote in *The Innocents Abroad* (1869), 'and entered a hearse belonging to the Grand Hotel de l'Europe. At any rate it was more like a hearse than anything else, though to speak by the card, it was a gondola.' He found it 'an inky, old rusty canoe with a sable hearse-body clapped on to the middle of it', and he took great exception to the gondolier's song, and quickly put a stop to it. 'Another yelp, and overboard you go!' he told him. But having stopped all that, in a few minutes they had 'swept gracefully out into the Grand Canal, and under the mellow moonlight the Venice of poetry and romance stood revealed . . . . Music came floating over the waters – Venice was complete.'

George Eliot, as might be expected, found that 'of all dreamy delights floating in a gondola along the canals and out into the lagoon is surely the greatest'. On the lagoon in a gondola when the sun was setting she would have liked the experience to have lasted for hours, she declared – it was the sort of scene in which she could most readily forget her own existence 'and feel melted into the general life'.

Robert Browning's long – and famous – poem, *In a Gondola*, does not, in fact, tell one much about the experience of being in a gondola, though it conveys something of Venice by night, gliding along the Guidecca – so far as one can make out. But all that kissing must have been tiresome for the gondolier. I am not sure, myself, that the gondola is so well designed for romantic love; the lovers,

I mean, are well and truly overlooked by the gondolier poised behind them. To the best of my knowledge and belief I have never been in a gondola; perhaps in the twenties, when I was there with my daughter, then a small child; certainly not in recent years, when I have always been alone; it is not anything you do solo, I think. Shelley thought that gondolas were 'like moths of which a coffin might have been the chrysalis'. Frederick Rolfe, 'Baron Corvo', had only eyes for the gracefulness of the gondoliers. For myself I am inclined to the uncomplicated view expressed by Horatio Brown in his imperishable *Life on the Lagoons* (1884) that the gondola is very beautiful, of swan-like grace, and 'a dear and lovely feature, the most familiar in the city of the sea'.

But the last word, I think, rests with J. E. Morpurgo, in the lovely picture book he did with Martin Hurlimann, called, simply, *Venice* (1964), when he says in his Introduction that 'the gondola is romantic Venice and will remain the symbol of Venice until the Grand Canal runs dry'.

6

TO FLORENCE
BY COACH

THERE was more to do in Venice – well, I suppose, there will
always be more to do in Venice – but after Chioggia-the-hard-way
I left for Florence, not from any nostalgia for Florence after forty-
five years, but from a desire to see Assisi and San Gimignano,
both of which I had – fantastically, it now seems – overlooked in
the twenties. I decided to go by coach rather than by train because
on the coach journey there were halts at Padua, Ravenna and
Bologna.

The young man from the Italian travel agents, Chiari Sommariva,
who had met me at the train on arrival – was it really only five days
ago? – came for me at 7.45 in the morning and took me by motor-
launch along the Grand Canal to the Piazzale Roma and the 'bus
terminal.

It is not all that wonderful a morning, but at least it is not
raining. The canal is busy and noisy with crowded *vaporetti*,
launches, and those strictly utilitarian 'gondolas' which serve
as ferries, laundry-boats, Coca-Cola boats, even refuse boats,
with the rubbish in black plastic bags to be dumped somewhere
out in the lagoon. Along the canal in the receding direction the
modern funnel of a ship is visible behind the Salute. We scoot under
the Accademia bridge and hurtle past the Palazzo Rezzonico and
take the short cut to the Piazzale Roma, and are there by eight
o'clock, which is half an hour too early. I am taken into an office and
my ticket is examined and an argument ensues between the 'bus
office clerk and the young man from the Chiari Sommariva. They
shout at each other and appear to be having the most fearful row,

but they are in fact merely amiably discussing some slight irregularity in the wording of the ticket – Italian discussions are apt to sound like rows. I am consulted, but I know nothing, I do not know anything, except that I am to travel to Florence on this day by this coach, and that these facts are set forth on the ticket. I have no idea what it is all about, but the 'bus office clerk clicks his tongue against his teeth and frowns, and the Chiari Sommariva young man tells me, reprovingly, that there is 'some confusion'. I assume an air of concern and throw in some tongue-clicking for full measure. The ticket is eventually returned to me more in sorrow than anger; the Chiari Sommariva young man takes his leave, and I am urged to take a seat in that dingy little office.

I do not, however, do anything so dismal, but wander about outside, where some pale sunshine has broken through the heavy grey clouds, and there are pigeons and people and that bustle which is life. There is a big coach which bears on its side the legend: Padua, Ravenna, Bologna, Firenze. I observe that there are already two passengers seated up in front and decided to join them, and return to the 'bus office for my baggage. Immediately I enter a slight girl approaches and inquires whether I am for Florence, and when I say yes she smiles and says, 'I am your hostess.' She looks very young, not more than about eighteen, though I learn later that she is twenty-two. A porter takes my typewriter and handgrip to the waiting coach and I clamber aboard. The other two passengers regard me with interest; they are middle-aged, a man and a woman. The woman is dark and squat and hook-nosed, and could be Jewish, I think, but on acquaintance she proved to be an American Catholic, of Italian extraction, like her husband. Many Italians have this deceptively 'Semitic' appearance, due to the hook noses and the dark complexions.

I say something to the young hostess, and the woman observes to her husband, 'She speaks English!'

Catching the husband's eye I smile and say, 'I *am* English!'

'Fine,' he says, pleasantly.

(There is nothing derisory about the American 'fine'. You

telephone someone and ask, 'How are you?' and they reply, 'Fine. How are you?' and you reply, 'Fine', and the other person says, 'That's fine!' It happened in the famous Transatlantic telephone call between Mr Harold Macmillan and General Eisenhower. 'How are you, Mr President?' inquires the British Prime Minister, very gentlemanly. 'Fine, Harold,' says General Eisenhower. 'How are you?' 'Fine,' says the British Prime Minister, not wishing to seem stand-offish. 'That's fine,' says the President. So everything is, uncomplicatedly and heartwarmingly, *fine*.)

With my baggage stowed away I settle into the front seat across from the Americans.

'You are the only passengers,' our hostess tells us.

The male American observes that 'they sure are running this trip at a loss!'

We head out over the motor road bridging the lagoon. There are Esso oil refineries across the water, and chemical works. At this side there is a huge car park. The outskirts of Venice are hideous. After a while we continue on a lower road, the *Autostrada* above us. We come to a toll bridge and a toll station, the bridge is overhead, and the four-lane motorway goes on forever. There are advertisement hoardings at each side as on the American motorways – there are many for Campari. We near Padua and fly over a motor-way and pass through another toll station. A signpost indicates *zona industriale*. Well, it is that all right; no need to signpost it. There are petrol stations at each side of the road. It could be a Greyhound coach New-York-to-Los-Angeles; but it is the CIAT coach Venice-to-Florence, and we are not approaching that city not-made-for-man, Los Angeles, but the fine old city of Padua, with arcaded streets, the Scrovegni chapel, Roman remains – and the famous Café Pedrochi which comes into Huxley's story, *Little Mexican*; the old Count was always sitting at the Café Pedrochi – 'But in Padua – where else?'

We stopped, inevitably, at the Scrovegni chapel, but I was glad of the opportunity to see the Giotto frescoes again unimpeded by any milling mob of schoolchildren. There were not many people in the chapel this time and I could take in the faded mural above the altar, the stone work above the choir stalls, the great barrel curve of the ceiling, its deep blue spangled with golden stars; this time it was possible to grasp the great sweep of the whole, and the realistic details of the frescoes. The American asks me if I can 'figure out the pictures'. I tell him, 'They depict the life of Jesus,' and 'Sure!' he says. He was, after all, brought up a Catholic. Perhaps he is merely trying to be helpful.

There is time for a quick look at the Eremitani church, thirteenth and fourteenth century, but it proves to be a huge barn of a place, more like a vast hall than a church, though there are some pleasant side chapels.

Approaching Ravenna we cross the River Po, and the Adriatic is pale and misty on our left. We are out of the industrial zone, now, and there is intensive agriculture – vineyards, sugar-beet, maize. Then industrialization again at the outskirts of Ravenna, with apartment blocks. The city lies in marshland and is subject to flooding, and dykes have been erected to protect it. The last big flood was in 1951 . . . so our young hostess told us, laying aside the embroidery with which she occupied herself when there was nothing of interest to import to her audience of three. As we trundle across the plain there are plantations of poplar trees, used in paper-making. Later there is a forest of umbrella pines. After the pines that succeed the poplars there are vineyards at each side of the road for a time, then poplars again. It is a little dull. On the coast there is the Marina di Ravenna, the Ravenna Riviera, the 'green coast of the Adriatic', with a pine forest running the length of it but we are not on the coast road.

As we approach the city our young hostess stands up to tell us that Ravenna has a population of 200,000, and is a 'cultural centre'. She is right about the culture, since Ravenna is famous for its fifth- and sixth-century Christian mosaics, but not about the population; she must have meant the entire province; the official brochure gives the population of the city of Ravenna as 128,000. (In 1961 it was 115,000.) But she is eloquent about Ravenna as the centre of early Christian religious art, and we listen respectfully. She concludes her little piece by telling us the name of the hotel at which we may lunch, if we choose, and shows us the menu. 'Only if you wish,' she insists. The price is 2,600 lire, which is nearly £2, and the meal is entirely Italian, and I do not wish. I plan to buy a sandwich, and snatch a Campari somewhere, and mooch – once we have 'done' the mosaics, which are the next item on the agenda.

The coach lumbers into the narrow streets of the city and comes to rest in a cul-de-sac under a high wall; the hotel where those who wish can take luncheon is just down the road from it. 'Here,' says our hostess, as we alight, 'you will go with another guide. He will show you the mosaics, and then conduct us back to the hotel, from which we are to depart for Bologna at two-thirty. OK?' It was OK.

What was not OK was the guide, a young man whose English was completely incomprehensible, the stresses all in the wrong places, reducing it all to gibberish. He marched ahead of us – and the party included a number of Americans from another coach – with an air of bored indifference, and we followed him to the church of San Vitale, described in the Blue Guide as 'the most precious example of Byzantine art extant in Western Europe'. It is sixth century and reached through a little garden of grass and trees. The interior is all marble and mosaics, and a splendour of pillars supporting the dome. We entered reverently and expectantly, and gathered round, all respectful and interested attentiveness, as the guide proceeded to hold forth. But with all the goodwill in the world – and I am sure that we did all bring the utmost goodwill, not to say effort, in the attempt to understand – we did not understand one word. After a few minutes people at the perimeter of the group began to move away and wander about on their own. I don't know whether the entire group dissolved, or whether a courteous few held on to the end, but certainly the group crumbled at the edges. I was gazing up at a wonderful mosaic above an arch – Christ and his disciples, so far as I could make out – when the American couple joined me. I said, 'I couldn't understand a word the guide said. Could you?' The woman said, 'Not a word!' Her husband declared, 'He might have been talking Chinese!'

We somehow all reassembled at a doorway of the church that led to the small building that is the Mausoleum of Galla Placidia, the sister of the Emperor Honorius. The Empress Placidia had the building erected in the middle of the fifth century; there are alabaster windows and most wonderful blue mosaics, and, as at the Scrovegni Chapel at Padua, the ceiling is strewn with golden stars. Fortunately the mosaics are readily comprehensible, so that the guide's gibberish did not matter, and we could stand round thim whilst he babbled and see everything, in that small space, from where we stood.

I spoke to some of the Americans from the other coach when we walked away across the grass and they all said that they had not understood a word of what the guide had said, but that at least where we had just been it hadn't mattered; we could see for ourselves what it was all about.

My advice to visitors to Ravenna is simply to go along to the Basilica di San Vitale, and thence to the Mausoleum of Galla Placidia, with a good guide book – such as the Blue Guide – in hand and 'figure it out' for themselves. For those with enough time there is a National Museum of Antiquities close to the church, which, with two Renaissance cloisters, should be interesting. There is also, of course, the Tomb of Dante, near the Piazza San Francesco, and at the corner of the Piazza San Francesco and the Via Ricci the site of the Palazzo Rasponi, Byron's first home in Ravenna, in 1819. Byron was fascinated by Ravenna, where he was involved in his romance with the young Countess Guiccioli. He rode in the pine woods beside the sea, and he loved the city with its narrow streets, its palaces, its basilicas with their tiled roofs. He worked there on *Don Juan* and on tragedies inspired by Venetian history, *Marino Faliero Doge of Venice*, and *The Two Foscari*. He stayed in Ravenna until the autumn of 1821, when he left for Pisa, where he rejoined the countess and her family, who have been expelled from Ravenna.

Whilst he was in Ravenna Byron compiled a *Ravenna Journal*, what he called a 'commonplace book'. It was issued for the first time in 1928 by the First Edition Club, with an introduction by Lord Ernle; I was fortunate in coming across a copy some years ago. In his introduction Lord Ernle says that the date of Byron's arrival in Ravenna, on June 10, 1819, is commemorated in an inscription over a café at the corner of the Piazza Byron and the Via Giuseppe Mazzini, formerly the Grand Albergo. Not all the *Ravenna Journal* was written in Ravenna some of it was written at Pisa, to which he went from Ravenna, in November, 1821. The journal ends with the 120th entry on May 18, 1822.

It is worth recalling that Byron did not leave Ravenna from choice, for he loved the city and preferred it to any other in which he had lived; but he was associated in the eyes of the authorities with the insurrectionary movements with which in 1820 and 1821 Italy was seething, and he was, in fact, politically involved, out of his innate passion for freedom; he was the champion of liberty – though it has been said of him that he was more of a king-hater than a people-lover. He made no secret of his revolutionary sympathies, and the police in Rome and Venice believed that 'many works, pamphlets, and dangerous writings which are in circulation have issued from the workshop of Lord Byron'. He was, moreover, associated – through his mistress, the young countess – with the Gamba family, and her father and brother were revolutionaries, and known as such. When at the end of July, 1821, 'a thousand people of the best families' in Ravenna were proscribed and exiled the countess's father and brother were among them, and she went with them into exile – she was by then separated from her husband and living with her father. It was apparently hoped, says Lord Ernle, that Byron would follow, 'but he remained on in Ravenna, trying to use his influence to mitigate the severity of the punishment inflicted on "high and low"', as well as on many personal friends'. A petition was sent 'by a number of the humbler inhabitants of the city' to the Papal Legate that he should be allowed to remain.

In August he was visited by Shelley, who had, apparently, an exhausting journey from Florence, travelling all night 'at the rate of two and a half miles an hour, in a little open carriage'. He arrived in Ravenna at ten o'clock at night, but, Iris Origo tells us, in her excellent book, *The Last Attachment* (1949), 'sat up talking with Byron until five the next morning'. During this visit Shelley suggested Pisa, where he was himself living, as a sanctuary for Byron and the Gambas, and to Pisa he somewhat reluctantly went, though his thoughts were already turning towards Greece.

I did not go in search of Byron when I mooched, munching a salami sandwich, in Ravenna – I had, in fact, forgotten that Milord was there – but it afforded me satisfaction to find a street named after Matteotti, the Via Giacomo Matteotti, with the tribute under the name, *Martire della Liberta*, 1885–1924. Was there really a time when we who were young-in-the-twenties saw nothing sinister in the Italian fascist movement under Benito Mussolini? The answer, extraordinary as it now seems, is that yes there was. It all seemed somehow romantic and youthful and hopeful. Young people returning from Italy in the mid-twenties regaled their friends with the fascist marching song. It was what we should nowadays call the 'fun thing'. Yet already there were reports of the 'castor-oil treatment' for political opponents, who were arrested and subjected to this beastliness. We knew about it and acknowledged – but too lightly – that that was bad. But when even Winston Churchill, in 1927, declared that if he had been an Italian he would have been wholeheartedly with the fascists in their 'struggle against the bestial appetites and passions of Leninism',* perhaps there was some excuse for us.

By way of the Via Giacomo Matteotti, which commemorates the murder of that brave socialist by Mussolini's blackshirts, I came through narrow cobbled streets where the only traffic was bicycles,

* *The Times*, January 21, 1927

to the large and splendid Piazza del Popolo, opening out of the small Piazza Giuseppe Garibaldi, with the tall Venetian columns at one end, and in the middle groups of men standing about talking, in the Italian way; or just standing about – which is also the Italian way.

Piazzas in Ravenna open out of each other like rooms in a palace. There was the small Piazza XX Settembre, and beyond it the Piazza J.F. Kennedy, mainly a car park. Then the Piazza del Duomo, with its basilica, and the tall round tower and small garden in front, with umbrella pines and ill-kept beds of geraniums, and a stunted palm, and a white, gold-crowned Virgin at the top of a pillar. I sit on a seat and make up some notes, but there is no peace here, away from the cobbled streets of the Piazza del Popolo area, for the cars circle round non-stop. The church, of course, is closed, it being midday. Writ large upon a wall is the slogan NO AL FASCISMO. I make a note that the streets round the Piazza del Popolo are all named after writers, historians, librarians.

Beyond the Piazza del Duomo there is the Piazza Monte Grappa, with a flower market; there is also a big covered market, with huge displays of fruit, vegetables, salads, cheeses, and meat and fish shops.

In this mooching from piazza to piazza I was singularly happy, feeling curiously light and free, for the first time since I arrived in Italy. I did not, of course, 'see Ravenna', but the little I saw of it gave me the feeling that this was my kind of a place. There are places in which one feels at ease, at home; places which, for no specific reason, speak to one's condition; for me Ravenna was such a place. Simply – 'I was happy there.'

On the road to Bologna – hideous with flyovers – the driver sings Italian songs. He has a melodious voice; it would be nice to understand the words, but it is not essential to enjoyment. We pass through an agricultural area, with orchards at either side of the road, and there are a great many sunflowers. The driver sings, and the young hostess concentrates on her embroidery. The three passengers, with nothing much to engage their attention, are inclined to doze.

As we draw near to Bologna there are misty hills, then blocks of flats, and industrialization . . . the usual hideous approach to a city. We turn off the six-lane motorway on to a lower road, humming with cars, and come soon to the handsome city centre, with fir trees, and terracotta-coloured houses, and arcades. Inscribed on a wall is *Viva Allende!* 'Bologna', our hostess tells us, gravely, 'is a strongly communist city!' (It has, in fact, I discovered later, a communist mayor.)

There are Roman remains beside a massive fountain with fine staircases, and at the base of a statue of Garibaldi, *Polizia Assassina*; there is the church of San Petronio, from the fourteenth century and still uncompleted. It is the largest church in Bologna and considered to be the finest example of Gothic brickwork in existence. It is certainly enormous. We alighted for an inspection. The interior is one of vast open spaces, with side chapels massive with huge marble pillars. There are enormous fluted red stone columns; and small, flimsy chairs standing little and lost half way in the open spaces, and one solitary elderly woman seated in this lonely wilderness, like a rock in a wide sea. Externally this unfinished church is very ugly in its top half, but in the lower half there is some beautiful stonework.

In the Piazza Nettuno there is a huge fountain with an enormous figure of Neptune and bronze figures of women squirting water from their ample breasts; they are supported by chubby cherubs, and there are pigeons galore, as at Ravenna.

There is a little time before the coach leaves and I go into a café and buy ice-cream, a huge dollop perched on a cornet, and this contributes to the enjoyment of mooching in the terracotta-coloured city.

There are posters expressing sympathy with the Russian dissidents; there are also hammers-and-sickles chalked on walls. On the Piazza Nettuno, where the great fountain is, there is the Palazzo di Re Enzo, where Enzo, King of Sardinia, was imprisoned for twenty-two years, until his death in 1272. It is used now as a place for meetings, and housed, then, a conference on smoking, at which it was possible to enrol for a course on how to give it up.

There are fir trees and acacia trees everywhere in this handsome city of terracotta-coloured brick, and there are hills close in behind. I was glad to have had a glimpse of Bologna, but it was, of course, hardly more than that.

Then we were off again, along the Highway of the Sun, to Florence. This romantically named motorway is an *autostrada* begun in 1960, from Milan to Reggio, in Calabria – in the toe of the boot of Italy, that is to say. There are the Apennines in the background and there are numerous tunnels. The road goes on and on through the wide beautiful valley, held in the golden evening light, with high wooded hills, fold upon fold of them, at either side. Back in from the *autostrada* lie the farmhouses and churches, villages and scattered dwellings, with outcrops of vineyards, that constitute the natural scene, and it is impossible not to reflect on how traumatic an experience for the country people must have been the cutting of the gigantic motorway through the peaceful countryside, and not to wonder how much natural beauty and immemorial way of rural life was sacrificed to this vast feat of engineering. And still the building goes on, ravaging the landscape with flyovers and still more tunnels.

We pass a modern church, like a huge tank, built in 1960; and the square block of a motel; but at last Florence looms in the distance, with the Duomo standing out in the plain, and the hills that hold Fiesole behind, and there are campaniles and towers . . . and the three passengers recover from the stupor of fatigue into which they have sunk and sit up and take an interest. We are *there*! Well – almost. And in fact not for quite a while, because the traffic in Florence is past belief. If any more cars go on the roads it must surely bring road transport to a stop. It took us half an hour to crawl into the city to the railway station and the 'bus terminal.

As we crawled along the Arno the American asked what river it was. There was a glimpse of the Ponte Vecchio, and of the Duomo but fifty years on it was all curiously unfamiliar. The river Arno, and the Ponte Vecchio and the Duomo, yes, of course, but Florence as one had remembered it from young-in-the-twenties, romantic exciting, . . . no, not really. This excruciating crawl along the Arno, this creep into the city, this monstrous constipation of cars . . . to-morrow the Duomo, the Piazza della Signoria, the Uffizi, the Boboli Gardens, the Pitti Palace, the lot, But meantime the car-jammed embankment, the choked streets, the creep, the crawl . . . and weariness. It is nine hours since we left Venice.

We finally reach the railway station and the 'bus terminal. The young man from Chiari Sommariva is there; a very efficient young man, who, it transpires, has learned his excellent English in Tewkes-bury, where he stayed in an old inn run by some friends of mine . . . He hands me over to Angelino, who is to be my driver, and scoots off ahead on his scooter. Duly we reach a green square, flanked at one end of a black and white church, the Piazza Santa Maria Novella, an oasis of quietness in the howling wilderness of traffic. The Minerva Hotel faces on to the piazza, and at the back looks across red roofs, interspersed with cypresses, to the hills on the lower slopes of which lies Fiesole, and to my great delight I am conducted to a little top-floor suite at the back.

In the little sitting-room there is a big vase of gladiolii with the compliments of the management. There is also a little refrigerator, which, upon investigation, proves to be very fully stocked – gin, vodka, whisky, brandy, even the common Coke. I settled for a quarter-bottle of Möet and Chandon – noting that there was still another, if required. It had been, after all, a very long day.

Above: *Florence, the Loggia dei Lanzi*: 'Cellini's Perseus holding aloft the Medusa's head.'

Below: The Palazzo Vecchio: 'Florence's most important civic building.'

Florence, Fort Belvedere: 'the ramparts afford a splendid view.'

The Boboli Gardens: 'begun in the sixteenth century and said to be one of the most magnificent gardens in the Italian style.'

7

FLORENCE REVISITED

IT is said that one must go to Venice for the paintings and to Rome for the architecture; I do not know, really, what it is one is supposed to go to Florence for, unless it is that it is the centre of art and learning, the 'Italian Athens'. When I went in the twenties, portable typewriter in one hand, young child in the other, I had no such high-falutin notions; I wanted to see something of Italy, and the obvious places were Venice, Florence, Rome, Naples. Florence I had found exciting because of the fabulous masterpieces of sculpture which just stood about at street corners as though they were of no account. Benvenuto Cellini, Donatello, Michelangelo, and the like. Then, too, there were the literary associations, with the Brownings, Shelley, George Sand. There was also Fiesole, on the hillside, at the other side of the city, and a wonderful view across the valley of the Arno. There was all that, and it was romantic.

Some forty-five years later I had no desire to revisit Fiesole; it was too much effort; but I did very much want to see the Duomo again, and the Piazza della Signoria, and the Cellini statue of Perseus, and to renew acquaintance with the Boboli Gardens. But about Fiesole it should be said that although on that occasion I could not be bothered, it is not really a difficult journey – just a matter of the No. 7 trolley bus from the Piazza San Marco, which is only up the Via Ricasoli from the Duomo, and there is a very fine view across the valley to Florence when you get there. The view back to Florence is really the only reason for going to Fiesole, though there are a few villas, including the Villa Landor, where that difficult man to end all difficult men, Walter Savage Landor, who strove with none, for none was worth his strife, according to his

E

celebrated poem, though he quarrelled with damn near everyone within his range, lived from 1829 until 1835, where he had the final quarrel with his wife and left her there and returned to England and a fresh set of rows. He was by then sixty; his family refused to make him an allowance unless he returned to Fiesole. Browning settled him in Siena, and he later moved to Florence, where he was visited by Swinburne, and where he died, in 1864, at the age of eighty-nine. He had his points, that fiery, cantankerous man; indeed he had; he cared as passionately as Byron about oppression; and he was a poet. Anyone visiting Florence for the first time should go to Fiesole; definitely. Whether they pay their respects to the Villa Landor or not.

My rediscovery of Florence cannot really be said to have begun with the Santa Maria Novella, for this corner of the city was new to me, but I went into this old Dominican church before setting out for the Duomo, because, since it was on my doorstep, it seemed the obvious thing to do. It was Sunday, and beggars were at the main doors, importuning people going in for Mass. Inside, though Mass was in progress, visitors wandered about. The interior is Gothic, and in the choir there are fifteenth-century frescoes by Ghirlandaio, and I am of those who always find ancient faded frescoes beautiful – provided there are not too many of them. Outside the church there are cloisters, with grass and trees. They are fourteenth century, and before I set out I was urged not to miss them. I looked at them several times, but my reaction was always negative. I like cloisters, but these seemed to me nothing much.

It is only a short walk from the Piazza Santa Maria Novella to the Piazza del Duomo, but it can be nervously exhausting, with so many roads to cross, and the difficulty of crossing them, and the narrow crowded pavements, and when you get there, of course, it is as milling with tourists as the Piazza San Marco, Venice, but in Venice there is at least no nightmare of cars and scooters circling nonstop around. But I had forgotten how wonderful is the façade of the Duomo, the Cathedral of Santa Maria del Fiore with its coloured marble, green, red, white, and how magnificent Brunelleschi's huge red cupola; it seemed to me almost more beautiful than the mosaic loveliness of Venice's San Marco. Despite the noise of the traffic and the density of the camera-slung tourists it had the same quality of something 'in a vision or a dream'. And the campanile – 'Giotto's tower', though in fact it was only begun by him in 1334, and was continued by Pisano nearly ten years later, worked on by Talenti five years after that, and finally completed by him in 1359; but, since there's no justice, it is 'Giotto's tower', reputedly one of the most remarkable campaniles in Italy, and surely one of the most beautiful.

In front of the cathedral there is the green and white marble Baptistery of San Giovanni, Dante's 'Bel San Giovanni', dedicated to St John the Baptist, the patron saint of the city. It is famous for its three bronze doors, two of them by Ghiberti, and the one facing the cathedral called by Michelangelo, 'the door of Paradise', depicting scenes from the Old Testament.

Only, of course, it's all too much to take in unless you are prepared to spend the whole day there on the Piazza del Duomo, and either you do that, it seems to me, studying it all 'in depth', or you just drift about, happily, enchanted by coloured marbles, impressed by great bronze doors, and carrying away with you an impression of something wonderful. I went into the cathedral, feeling in duty bound, but it is vast and bare, full of monuments and busts, and, as in almost all Italian churches, I felt quite unable to cope. For those interested in such things, you can ascend into the dome, 463 steps, and be rewarded by what the Blue Guide calls 'an incomparable panorama' extending over the whole city to the hills beyond; similarly with the campanile, 414 steps, which 'commands a succession of interesting views'. This astonishing complex is, of course, the centre, the very heart of Florence, and the campanile and the great red cupola its landmarks from afar.

I wanted to go next to the Piazza della Signoria, but in spite of much consultation of the street map got lost and found myself in the Piazza della Repubblica, which is a very large square, and in the Via Roma, off it, I had been puzzled by what seemed to me more than Sunday-strolling crowds but a mass-formation density of young men, and people were peering out from the doorways of shops and cafés. The young men seemed to be marching, rather than strolling, and to be six or more abreast. I have a fear of crowds and I wanted to get away from the Via Roma, but in trying to do so came into the Piazza della Repubblica, and here there was a great crowd of young men, and police with rifles, with fixed bayonets, and steel helmets, and shields over their faces. The young men drummed a tattoo on the bonnets of cars, and once they started a slow handclap. They stood smiling, jeering, occasionally shouting slogans, waiting; waiting for something to happen. One young man threw some coins at a posse of police; but nothing happened. Someone had only to throw a stone, I thought. But no one threw a stone; they all just stood there, drumming on the car bonnets, occasionally clapping, jeering – trying to provoke the police into action, but the steel-helmeted men with the fixed bayonets stood impassively. Presently an officer moved them off and they marched briskly away, in good order. The young men clapped and jeered and drummed on the bonnets of cars, and a good time was had by all.

I inquired about it when I got back to the hotel in the evening, and was told, with a shrug, that it was a communist demonstration. 'They are encouraged by the Chinese exhibition now in the city. They are students.' That they were students was said dismissively, contemptuously; for myself I do not think the international student movement negligible. I was anyhow very interested. Later I discovered that the Chinese exhibition was out at the Belvedere, along the Arno, on the Pitti Palace side, not far from the Boboli Gardens. Almost everywhere on my Italian journey I saw chalked up on walls and at the bases of statues anti-police slogans, usually describing them as assassins. On the coach from Venice to Florence I had a good deal of talk with our young hostess. She told me that she was engaged to be married, and she had a problem because her fiancé was against the Church, whereas she was still a practising Catholic. I asked whether many young people still went to Mass; she said not so many; especially not the young men; she added, significantly, 'They are more interested in politics!' I read in an article in *The Times*,* before I left for the Italian journey, that little more than a third of the Italian population goes to Mass every week, and that about thirteen million have lost the habit altogether. The article was by the Rome correspondent, and the figures are from a survey by the Doxa Institute. That the young men are 'more interested in politics' seemed to be borne out not only by the demonstration in the Piazza della Repubblica but by the numerous hammer-and-sickle signs scrawled on walls and on the plinths of statues in streets and squares. I am told they are even more in evidence in Rome, where the non-attendance at Mass is even higher.

I made my way along the Via dei Calzaiuoli, dreadful with traffic, crowds, noise, to the Piazza della Signoria, the 'political and historical centre of Florence'.† I had remembered an 'arcade', the Loggice dei Lanzi, with sculptures, notably Cellini's Perseus holding aloft the Medusa's head, and a fountain, and some steps upon which to sit and survey the whole splendid scene; and, of course, the great gaunt Palazzo Vecchio, with its high tower, the city's most important civic building. It is all, obviously, still there, and why I failed to recapture the excitement with which some forty-five years ago I had first set eyes on it all I simply do not know. The Duomo had proved to be more beautiful than I had remembered it; but the Piazza della Signoria seemed only grey, and somehow enclosed, and it was dense with tourists, and neither the Neptune fountain nor Cellini's masterpiece could restore that first fine careless rapture; whilst the Vecchio Palace seemed only stark and ugly. Memory plays one tricks; and age is the ultimate betrayer. There was the Uffizi Gallery, the most wonderful collection of paintings in the world – all those fantastically beautiful Botti-

---

*August 17, 1973

† A plan to repave the piazza in brick, as it was at the time of the Renaissance, has been held up by the discovery by excavating workmen of what are believed to be the remains of the city's Byzantine walls below the sqaure (*The Times*, January 13, 1974).

cellis – and I remembered, vividly, the excitement with which I had first entered the Uffizi, but I had no desire to revisit it now, though very well I remembered *Primavera*, and *The Birth of Venus*.

I continued on to the Ponte Vecchio, and there all was as I had remembered it, with the little shops at each side; the only change is one which is to the good – which usually change is not – and that is that it is closed to traffic, and has been for the last ten years. Yet it is, in fact, changed, for in 1944 the old houses at each end were blown up, in the retreat, and some of the shops were damaged by the 1966 flood; memory, however, is not concerned with detail but only general outline, and the Ponte Vecchio, even minus some of pre-Second-World-War memory; only finer, being now a pedestrian thoroughfare.

At the other side I stopped at a café and had the usual midday Campari and sandwich, then continued along the Via Guicciardini to the Pitti Palace, fifteenth–sixteenth century and quite as ugly as one had remembered. The huge courtyard in front is full of cars and tourist coaches, but because the palace itself is so relentlessly ugly it hardly matters. My business, however, was not with the Pitti Palace – 'plain but majestic', says the Blue Guide – but with the Boboli Gardens behind, 'one of the most magnificent gardens in the Italian style', begun in the sixteenth century. I remembered, really, nothing about it, except that when you visited the Pitti Palace you went as a matter of course into the Boboli Gardens behind. Whether I found the gardens romantic in my youth I do not now remember, but certainly they are no place for the elderly, with all the steps and steep slopes leading up to the succession of terraces. Apart from that I found them dull, as formal gardens tend to be, and, on that grey day with the wind whipping up the dust from the loose gravel, singularly arid. At the top there is a fine view out over Florence, all red roofs and the great cupola and the campanile, and the tower of the Vecchio Palace, and the low hills that are the background for the city.

The gardens were made by the Medici family when they acquired the Pitti Palace in 1549 and some of the land surrounding it, which they purchased from various families, amongst them the Bogoli, or Bogolini family, whence the name for the gardens, Boboli, is believed to derive.

Across from the Piazza Pitti there is the Piazza San Felice, where, at number nine, the fifteenth-century Casa Guidi, Robert Browning and his wife lived from 1848 until her death in 1861. The house is open to the public – oddly – from 6 p.m. until midnight. It faces the church, and when the Brownings lived there – in a furnished apartment – the piazza was 'a place of fairs, pageants and parades'. They were happy there, and in her *Casa Guidi Windows* Elizabeth Barrett Browning wrote lyrically of the 'golden Arno' shooting its way 'through Florence' heart beneath her bridges four'. Frances Winwar, in her biography of the Brownings, *The Immortal Lovers* (1950), said that Casa Guidi 'meant home, health, happiness and the joyous labour of their poetry to the Brownings'. Though, to be sure, in 1851 they let the place and went to England. Their first home in Florence, after they left Pisa, was a furnished apartment near Santa Maria Novella; they left it because the windows did not get the sun, and though they had taken out a lease for six months Mrs Browning was so unhappy there that when they found the sunny apartment in the Casa Guidi they took out another lease there, where, says Frances Winwar, they had 'only to stand at the windows to look out on beauty – the vivid life of the square from the front balcony, the flowering orange and camellias from the rooms that faced the garden'.

There were not many people in the Boboli Gardens that grey Sunday afternoon in late September, only a few here and there, sitting on steps eating sandwiches, it being noon. No one sat at the tables in the garden of the little café. The sky was heavy with dark rain clouds, ominous above the city.

The rain set in when I reached the other side of the Ponte Vecchio, where the cars streamed non-stop along the Arno, grey in the grey light.

8

ASSISI AND PERUGIA

It had been my intention simply to take a tour to Assisi, but the efficient young man who had met me on arrival in Florence had had an itinerary session with me when we got to the hotel and had been startled and dismayed when I had said, carelessly, that as for Assisi and Perugia, I understood there was a tour, and the coach would pick me up at the hotel. He demanded, why should I go by coach, with forty-five other people, when a private car and driver were at my disposal? His instructions from London, he said, firmly, were that I would travel by private car to Assisi and Perugia on Monday, and by the same car, with the same driver, Angelino, to San Gimignano and Siena on Tuesday. Why should I wish to travel by coach? Difficult to explain that one didn't really want the VIP treatment all the time, and that when you were travelling alone it was sometimes nice to be with other people. But 'London' was the good friend who had arranged the whole thing, and when a friend lays on a private car and driver it is nothing less than churlish to insist on going by coach – with forty-five other people.

So I set out with the good Angelino at 8.30 a.m., for the long drive to Assisi. We left Florence by the ancient gateway, the Porta Romana, and were soon on the motorway, and it was the Autostrada del Sole again, the Highway of the Sun, but this time in the rain. There were flyovers, and huge lorries thundering past, and a hoarding indicating *Zona Industriale*. There were outcrops of industrialization, factories and works, scattered amongst agricultural lands, olive groves and vineyards; then blocks of flats, and pylons, and a sign which says Arezzo, but because we are on a motorway we do not pass through this ancient chief city of Tuscany; it is somewhere out there, on the left, on a hillside, hidden, and we continue with the flyovers, the scattered industrialization, and a featureless landscape, with the Arno, narrow, down below. Angelino draws my attention to a dam constructed after the great flood of 1966.

There are SOS signs at intervals along the route, and I am puzzled and intrigued, but Angelino explains that they are nothing to do with the international call for help – they are to do with Esso. There are oil tankers and lorries zooming past, some of the lorries stacked high with new cars. There is a toll station, and at weary last we turn off the autostrada and on to a National Road, busy with cars in both directions, but a relief after hours on the motorway The countryside remains featureless, but at least the rain had stopped and some watery sunshine emerged.

It is pleasant to drive through the attractive village of Passignano, a summer resort beside Lake Trasimeno, which is wide and reedy and has three islands. Angelino tells me that it was the scene of Hannibal's victory over the Romans in 217 BC. 'Unfortunately for the Romans', says Angelino, 'many of them died in the lake.' The lake itself is dying, it seems, becoming choked with peat and weeds and reverting to marsh.

We pass through the little town of Magione, with old houses, and acacia trees in the main street, and at the other side enter a broad valley; there are vineyards, the vines heavy with great clusters of black grapes, and Perugia comes into view on a hillside, to the left, climbing to a ridge. 'It is famous for very fine wool, and for chocolate', says the ever-informative Angelino. It is also famous for its porcelain – and its Etruscan walls.

We are back on the motor road, with petrol stations and an endless procession of cars, and, inland, twelve-storey blocks of flats. 'Another bypass is being made down below,' says Angelino.

It is ten-thirty and we have been travelling for two hours, though it seems much longer. But now it is only twenty-seven kilometres to Assisi, and the clouds have cleared and the sun shines.

The little town is soon visible on the lower slopes of Monte Subasio, rising from the Umbrian plain and surmounted by a fortress. There is a foreground of vineyards, olive groves, cypresses, and a background of gently rising hills. In the valley, away over to the right, is a great church, with a dome. 'Santa Maria degli Angeli', says Angelino, and we drove on and up into the city, through a great gateway in the walls, and come to rest in the Piazza Santa Chiara – St Clare – with its church, and it is eleven o'clock.

The square, with the flying buttresses of the church, looking out over the broad valley, was quiet and beautiful. It all looked wonderful in the warm sunshine, and after the long and mainly dull drive I was so very glad to *be* there, and I had, very much, wanted to visit Assisi, having a great respect for both St Francis and his great friend St Clare, but now that I was actually there I had the sudden panicky feeling that it was all going to prove too much. 'It's all *churches*!' I had been warned, and it is . . . but incapable as I am of suspending disbelief when it comes to miracles and such, I nevertheless liked Assisi and was moved by it.

When the good Angelino had parked the car in the Piazza Santa Chiara he conducted me to a small office, where I was introduced to a good-looking and youngish English woman – 'Your English guide!' Angelino cried, triumphantly.

I shook hands with my fellow countrywoman, whom I instantly liked, and we went outside and stood by a low wall looking out over the wide, lovely plain, and talked a little. She inquired what brought me to Italy and I explained about the book, and I learned that she was married to an Italian and was living in Assisi – 'in a modern house' – with her husband and children. I told her that I had long had a wish to visit Assisi as some years ago I had written about St Francis and St Clare.* I asked her about the Zeffirelli film of St Francis, which I had not seen, but had read about and did not, as a result, feel attracted to. I gathered that it opened with a back view of Francis naked. . . . Well, yes, but it was all right; she was non-committal. It had been made in Assisi, and a number of the local

*In *Rebels' Ride, the Revolt of the Individual,* 1964.

people had been engaged for crowd work, but the film had had to be cut, and so none of the locals who had expected to appear in the film of St Francis did in fact appear; which was disappointing.

Well, so. We turned away from the sunny wall and got to work. We began, naturally, with the church of St Clare, a few steps from where we stood.

It is Romanesque and thirteenth century, red- and white-striped. The interior is simple, with faded, beautiful frescoes of the school of Giotto, and a vaulted, painted ceiling similarly attributed. In the Chapel of the Sacrament there is, behind glass, the painted Crucifixion that spoke to St Francis at San Damiano, the convent of the Poor Clares, outside the city walls, bidding him go forth and repair the church. The church contains, also, the tomb of St Clare, which is a glass case, illuminated, in which lies the body of the saint, found under the high altar in 1850, and alleged to be undecayed by the passage of some six centuries. The face of the saint is, curiously, as black as the nun's robes that clothe – whatever they do clothe. On the head there is a wreath of white artificial flowers. In the church, above, Poor Clare nuns, behind grilles, their faces so heavily veiled that not even the eyes are discernible, explain about the 'incorruptible body' of the saint and hand out leaflets in English, French, German, Italian, as required.

We went next to the twelfth-century Cathedral of San Rufino, off the Via Rufino, in the oldest part of the city. It is very beautiful, with rose windows. St Rufino was the first bishop and martyr of Assisi. The church contains the font at which both St Francis and St Clare were baptized, and there is a lady chapel with a very beautiful Virgin and Christ in an alcove.

The Via di San Rufino leads up and on to the main square of the town, the Piazza del Commune, where there is the Roman Temple of Minerva, now the baroque church of Santa Maria – the temple, which dates from Augustus, is, in fact, inside the church. It is ornate, with Corinthian columns, and a great deal of gold and marble. Externally steps rise between pillars to the entrance, and there is said to be a Roman forum below the present pavement of the square. There are Roman remains, a theatre and an amphitheatre, behind the cathedral of San Rufino, at the top of the lane.

It is very pleasant walking about in Assisi, if you don't mind hilliness and steps – there is not much level walking, except in the squares. As I observed to my companion at one point, as we ascended a steep lane, it is no town for the elderly, for it is all steps and streets of steps, and steep, narrow, cobbled lanes. We came by way of narrow streets and flights of steps to the Via San Francesco, which is wider, and on the level, and leads to the great church. It is a street of old houses, and at number eleven there is the Oratorio dei Pelligrini, the pilgrims' oratory; in 1431 it was a hospital where pilgrims were lodged; it is now an intimate little chapel, with faded, beautiful fifteenth-century frescoes.

All this I much enjoyed, but as we approached the great basilica, with its Upper and Lower Church, the most important monument in Assisi, I began to feel scared. So far it had all been easy – comprehensible; the Basilica of San Francesco could, from its sheer importance, prove to be too much, I feared. But there it was, majestically looming, with a Gothic portal and a rose window and a square campanile, all thirteenth century. It is tremendously impressive, but inside it is not at all daunting, but light and beautiful, with lovely delicate vaulting, and starry blue-painted ceilings, with paintings by Cimabue, and along the walls frescoes of the life of St Francis by Giotto and his disciples. There are also frescoes of Old Testament history – 'most likely by Pietro Cavallini and his pupils'.

The Lower Church is reached through a fifteenth-century Renaissance porch. It is dim, and it is hard to believe that it is not the crypt of the Upper Church, but it is a church in its own right, and from it descends a staircase of the crypt in which there is the tomb of St Francis, a raised stone coffin, 'rendered inaccessible in the fifteenth century as a precaution against Perugian raids, and rediscovered in 1818'. There is really nothing much to say about it; you can walk all round it, and, if I remember rightly, mount some steps for a closer view, but it is unremarkable. St Francis was not originally interred here, but in the church of San Giorgio, and a fund was started in 1228, two years after his death, for a memorial church, and the foundation stone was laid by Pope Gregory IX the day after the canonization ceremony. In another two years this church, the Lower Church, was completed, and the body of the saint removed to it. The campanile was completed in 1239.

From the chapel of St Antony there is the entrance to the cloisters, in the fifteenth century a cemetery for the monks, now merely cloistral, with tall cypresses and a cool green peace.

After all this – and it was a lot – it was lunch time. The guide was anxious to get back to her house and the children coming home from school; she was also anxious that I, her charge, should lunch well. In vain I protested that a Campari-and-sandwich at any old caff suited me well enough, as I would be dining in style at the hotel in Florence in the evening, and one meal a day was all I reckoned to have. She persisted; there was a very good restaurant at a hotel on the hillside just outside Assisi, with wonderful views. It would be interesting and pleasant for me. She explained to Angelino where it was. But Angelino, most amiable of drivers, was not happy with the idea; he protested that it was too far out, and that he would never find it, and there were plenty of places in the town that would suit the signora. There was some argument in Italian. But it transpired that the house of the guide was on the way to this restaurant, which was indeed but a step beyond, and since she must be taken to her house, and that immediately, to feed her hungry children . . . . So we drove up and out through a great gateway, and the guide descended above a valley, her house on the hillside just below, and Angelino and I drove on along the road winding round a hillside.

We did not come to any hotel or restaurant and Angelino began to complain. Where was this place? *Mamma mia*, were there not plenty of restaurants in Assisi, that we must drive out into the countryside? I agreed that indeed there were, and I did not want a heavy meal; only a drink and a sandwich at a bar or café, since I would be eating in the evening, at the hotel. 'If we find this restaurant it will cost you two thousand lire – *minimum*!' Angelino declared. 'It is too much,' I said. 'Let us return to Assisi!'

This we did, and depositing me in the main square Angelino said, 'Here you can have a drink and a sandwich. Also you can wash your hands.'

Yes, indeed. It had occurred to me that it was about time I 'washed my hands.'

Angelino did not abandon me in the square. He settled me on the terrace of a café. He even gave the order to the waiter – for a Campari-soda, and a sandwich and for the signora to be shown where she could wash her hands.

All things were accomplished, and in an hour's time Angelino collected me and we drove back to the great gateway and collected the other English signora.

It was explained to her, in both English and Italian, that we had been unable to find the hotel – but in neither language that we had not really tried very hard – and that I had been perfectly happy to rest and take refreshment at a café on the main square. The signora was not, to give her her due, all that concerned; she had made a recommendation, and if it had not been followed up it was not her responsibility; her responsibility was to get her fellow country-woman to the convent of San Damiano, and then on to Perugia, taking in Santa Maria degli Angeli, St Mary of the Angels, that other great Franciscan shrine, en route. There was a lot to do.

So we drove to the Convento di San Damiano, outside the walls of the city, to the south. It was here that Francis of Assisi heard the call to renounce the world and rebuild the church, and here that he duly installed his friend, Clara Sciffi, also of Assisi, after introducing her into his Order, and it was here, after living happily for forty years or so in Franciscan poverty, she died in 1253, as abbess of the Franciscan order of the Poor Clares, which she founded in 1212. In addition to their poverty, the nuns were veiled, enclosed, and silent. Poor Clares indeed!

The convent is a bare and simple building, essentially Franciscan.

Up some stone stairs you come out into a little patio – St Clare's garden. In a corner there is a wrought-iron ornament made by blind people to celebrate the occasion of St Francis being made in 1926 the patron saint of Italy.

Up another flight of stone steps from the little garden there is the nuns' dormitory, where St Clare died. A vase of Madonna lilies marks the spot where her bed stood; and a similar vase of lilies marks the spot where she sat in the refectory. There is a little chapel in which there is a very beautiful crucifix, showing Christ smiling, viewed from one angle, and looking sorrowful, viewed from another. There are cloisters, with a well in the middle, and potted plants, and arum lilies, and swallows' nests in specially provided boxes – provided because until they were they nested all over the place and made the most terrible mess. There are lovely tiled roofs, and there is a wonderful silence. Finally there is the window, looking out over the courtyard, to the road, at which St Clare stood, holding the Host aloft, when Frederick II's Saracen troops assaulted the town, and the Muslims, superstitiously dismayed by this Christian apparition, retreated. It is a pleasant tale – and feasible.

I liked San Damiano; it is simple and Fransciscan and comprehensible. Would I like to visit Santa Maria degli Angeli? Well, yes, I would, not so much as a Franciscan shrine as because it looked so strange, sitting out there, down below, isolated in the plain.

Franciscan shrine it of course inescapably is, since St Francis died there, though the church is itself sixteenth century. It was built to cover the little oratory, the Porziuncola, which was founded by hermits from Jerusalem in the fourth century, was restored by St Benedict in the sixth, and became the first centre of the Franciscan Order; and it was here that Clare was received by Francis into his Order; here at the foot of the altar he cut off her hair, invested her with the Franciscan habit, and accepted her vows of poverty, chastity and obedience. Here, too, took place that meeting she had so desired, when they would eat together, sit down together at table as the old friends they were. He visited her many times at St Damian's and gave her religious instruction, but, as recorded in *The Little Flowers*, never would he grant her the consolation of this, her dearest wish. Finally he was persuaded by his companions that he was being too severe, and wanting in divine charity, by this persistent refusal. They urged that it was after all but a small grace she entreated, she who was so holy a virgin and beloved of God, and who, through his preaching at the Porziuncola, had forsaken the 'pomps and riches of this world' and embraced poverty. She was his spiritual plant, and even if she asked a greater grace than this so humble one he should grant it.

To this Francis replied, with characteristic humility, that if it seemed good to them that he should do this then it seemed good to him, and he and Clare would have the repast in the Porziuncola, that she might be the more consoled, 'for long hath she been shut up in St Damian's, and it will profit her to behold the friary of St Mary, where her hair was shorn and she became the spouse of Jesus Christ; there will we break bread together in the name of God'. On the appointed day Clare left St Damian's with one companion and journeyed to the Porziuncola, and some of the friars showed her round the friary 'until the hour of the repast was come'.

As I observed in *Rebels' Ride*, it would have been interesting to know what the repast consisted of, but we are told only that Francis 'made ready the table on the bare ground, as he was wont to do', and when Clare and her companion were seated, and he and one of his own companions, then the other friars took their places, but not much eating was done, for with the first dish Francis began to discourse 'so sweetly, so loftily, so wondrously' about God that they were too rapt to eat, and so bright a radiance enveloped the Porziuncola and the surrounding woods that the place seemed to be on fire and people came running to extinguish the flames. 'But when they came to the friary and found nothing burning they entered within and found St Francis and St Clare and all their companions seated round that humble table and rapt in the contemplation of God', and when they understood that it was a divine fire they had seen from afar 'they departed with great consolation in their hearts and holy edification'. As for Clare and

Above: Assisi, the convent of San Damiano: '... cloisters with a well in the middle, and potted plants, and swallows' nests in specially provided boxes ...'

Below: The Piazza del Commune: '... with the Roman temple of Minerva, now the church of Santa Maria.'

Assisi, the convent of San Damiano: 'the window at which St. Clare stood, holding the Host aloft, when the Saracens assaulted the town.'

San Gimignano: 'the towers seem to grow out of the old houses.'

her companion, and the friars, they felt so well comforted with spiritual food that they 'took little head of corporeal food'. The reference to the company sitting round 'that humble table' appears to contradict the earlier reference to the table on the bare ground, unless it simply means that the meal was taken out in the open. Anyhow, the good sisters at St Damian's, the narrative continues, were very relieved when Clare returned, for they had feared Francis might send her away to another convent, as he had already sent her sister, Agnes.

The church of St Mary of the Angels which enshrines the tiny stone chapel that Francis repaired is huge, and grandiose, with chandeliers, and massive marble and baroque splendours; there are electric candles round the ancient stone walls, and there is a beautiful altar with della Robbia decorations, and a Chapel of the Rose, sentimental with a statue of St Francis holding a bowl of roses on which white doves perch. The chapel marks the site of the hut in which Francis lived whilst he worked on restoring the oratory, though some say it marks the site of the cave in which he lived. The Cappella del Roseto, to give it its Italian name, is decorated with frescoes by Tiberio d'Assisi, a pupil of Perugino, and is named from the thornless roses of St Francis which bloom in the adjoining garden – thornless, according to the legend, because Francis, physically combating the Devil, fell into a rose bush, or a rose bed; the Devil was ousted, and the roses that bloomed there were thornless forever after. . . . It is a pleasant tale, like the reason why the robin has a red breast, only to no saint has there been such an accretion of sentimentality as to the gentle yet strong, strong yet gentle, Francesco Bernardone of Assisi.

G. K. Chesterton, who in 1923 wrote a biography of St Francis of Assisi, wrote in his autobiography in 1936 that when he first went to Florence he had only a confused impression that the city was full of English ladies, all Theosophists; but that when he had been to Rome ('in more senses than one', he wrote) he saw that this was not quite fair, and that 'there really is a sympathy between English and Italian culture', and 'really something warm-hearted

F

and romantic gilding those stark cliffs that look across the plain to Perugia'. He added that 'the English do appreciate St Francis as they do not appreciate Pascal or the Curé d'Ars. . . . They have some comprehension of medievalism in Italy.'

Across the plain, then, to Perugia, with a last lovely view of Assisi on its hillside. I would have liked to have visited the hermitage of St Francis, to which he liked to retire for meditation, small, and stone-built, in a setting of wooded hills, but one cannot do everything in a day, and I left Assisi feeling very strongly that it was a place to *stay* in – for days, weeks, as long as one's time and money permitted. There are always places to which one would like to return; for me Assisi is one.

But we were on the road to Perugia, and Perugia is a good place, too, though it did not move me as Assisi did. It stands like Assisi on a hillside, in fact upon a group of hills, like Rome, above the Tiber. It was founded by the Etruscans, whose walls still stand, and we entered the city through a massive ancient gateway, but round the corner there was a supermarket, and the scooters roaring past – as they do, alas, in the narrow streets of Assisi. But there is this to be said for Perugia – amongst the many things to be said for this beautiful and ancient city – and that is that there is a main street for pedestrians only.

There was so little time in Perugia that I have no clear picture of it as a city, but I have notes of, and remember, the beautiful Piazza Quattro Novembre, said to be the most beautiful in the city, with its lovely fountain, late thirteenth century, the Fontana Maggiore, with its centrepiece of three nymphs by Pisano. (But does it really have to be so brutally fenced round nowadays with iron palings?) Across the piazza is the unfinished Cathedral of San Lorenzo, where, said my guide, at least five popes were elected – the idea of the conclaves of cardinals for the election of popes originated in Perugia, it would seem (I say 'it would seem', for I know nothing of such matters, and do but report what I was told). Here, too, is the Palazzo dei Priori, the Palace of the Priors, now the Palazzo Communale, late

thirteenth century, completed in 1443. The priors were the govern-
ing body of the time, as the doges were in Venice. There is a great
deal of interest in the palace if you have the time to devote to it,
which I hadn't, unfortunately; there is, for one thing, an important
collection of Umbrian paintings.

If you have only a few hours at your disposal what you are likely
to be shown is the Benedictine church of St Peter, and the – to
me – bewildering and rather frightening – Rocca Paolina. The
main structure of the church is twelfth-century; it is full of marble,
and pagan columns; there are sixteenth-century choir stalls, marvellously carved, and beautiful inlaid work, like paintings, in the
doors. There is much else, including a Pietà by Perugino, and a
painting of Christ on the Mount by Guido Reni. All that was fine;
in every Italian church, if you are conscientious – which I reckon
to be – you bring such comprehension and appreciation as you
can to bear.

But the Rocca Paolina is another matter. It appears to be a walled
city within the walled city of Perugia, but roofed over. At the time
I did not at all understand it, but I have since read that at the com-
mand of Pope Paul III, in the mid-sixteenth century, a whole
medieval quarter of the city was vaulted over. The idea was to
create a fortress at the heart of the city which would serve also as a
prison, and many princely homes and churches were sacrificed to
this end. It was a monstrous idea, and in 1848 the people rose
against it and destroyed it. The entrance to this sinister place is
through the huge arch of the Porta Marzia in the massive Etruscan
walls.

Inside, you come at once to the Via Baglioni, named after the
distinguished Baglioni family, and once a public road in the city.
The princely home of the Baglionis was one of those sacrificed for
the creation of this citadel. It is somehow sinister, because it is an
inner city in which there is no daylight, no sky over, and a street
lamp hung from a wall creates an eerie impression amongst the dark
arches and deep shadows.

For me it was like a crypt, with its grim walls, and its streets going off into darkness; a place to get out of. It was like a stage set, unreal, but sinister.

It was a relief to get out again into the sunlight and return to the Porta San Pietro, with cedars and beds of bright flowers, and a view out over the fertile plain, and a feeling of height – and light.

My visit to Perugia ended there – with very much more to see, including some wonderful Perugino paintings in the National Gallery of Umbria, but I was glad to have had the glimpse; and the Rocca Paolina was an experience.

9

SAN GIMIGNANO

WITH my passion for walled towns and cities San Gimignano was high on the agenda for my Italian journey. It is not much more than an hour's drive from Florence, and the route lies through Chianti country. The scenery, however, is not of much interest – ploughed land, with scattered factories, vineyards, low hills in the near distance; pleasant but unspectacular. San Gimignano is soon visible on its hill-top.

But first comes the small town of Poggibonsi, with ugly blocks of flats with washing hanging from the balconies, and an American-style main street. There is a warehouse for the Chianti wine, by the sale of which, I gather from Angelino, it chiefly lives. In the centre of the town there are umbrella pines and chestnut and plane trees, and a busyness of traffic, and women with shopping bags. There is a fifteenth-century castle and a thirteenth-century church, and medieval houses; but we drove straight through the town centre and out the other side into Chianti country again, with vineyards lush with black grapes. There are vines growing on trellises, which, says Angelino, is a modern idea. There are olive groves, but the olives are only 'kitchen olives, for cooking', says Angelino, 'not for eating'. As an inveterate olive eater I think this a pity. San Gimignano remains visible on its hill-top.

We enter through the San Giovanni gate, said to be the town's finest, and enter a narrow street with no pavements 'forbidden to the 'bus', says Angelino, and adds, 'San Gimignano lives by tourists, and through another gate come into the main square, the Piazza della Cisterna, with its 'cistern', the well, in the middle.

The Blue Guide declares that San Gimignano has preserved its medieval appearance more completely than any other town in

Tuscany, or perhaps in Italy'. More than Assisi? I would not have thought so. But then I liked Assisi, whereas I did not really like San Gimignano, which seemed to me a tourist trap, with every other house a souvenir shop, and the feeling of it all as a show-place.

Anyhow, we parked the car, and the official guide, who had been arranged for me, loomed up, and led the way into the adjoining square, the Piazza del Duomo, to begin the sightseeing with the twelfth-century cathedral, the Collegiata. The guide did literally lead the way, walking ahead of me the whole time, his hands clasped behind his back, his head down, as though leading a funeral procession. I tried several times to walk level with him and initiate some rudimentary conversation that would keep him by my side, but it was no use; he would deal briefly with any question or comment I might come up with then deliberately stride out ahead. leaving me trekking along again in the rear.

In this fashion we reached the cathedral, the interior walls of which are covered by frescoes. There is a great deal of Carrera marble, and there are microphones up at the high altar, which is fifteenth century and which the guide calls 'this beauteous tabernacle'. In the Chapel of Santa Fina there is a painting by the saint, who died when she was fifteen. The walls are covered with frescoes by Ghirlandaio depicting her life. Santa Fina is 'the saint of the violet' and the patron saint of the town. The legend has it that at her death angels rang the bells of the town and violets suddenly flowered on all the towers, a miracle said to be renewed every year. Well, the miracle of spring is renewed every year, including the violets, though where a violet root might get a foothold on those tall square towers that are the chief feature of San Gimignano it's hard to see. A finger of the saint is buried at the back of the chapel altar. And there are frescoes, frescoes, frescoes; and nearby is the Museum of Sacred Art where there are still more. There is a view over the square from the museum to the towers, which seem to grow out of the roofs of old houses, and round the tops of which crows circle endlessly. There are a great many tourists milling about down below and their voices rise on the still air. Opera is given sometimes in the piazza in the summer, says the guide. There is a collection of sixteenth- and seventeenth-century pharmacy jars; and a plaque to Dante, who came here from Florence – in the Palazzo del Popolo across the square there is the Sala del Consiglio where he is supposed to have delivered his appeal. In the museum there is a 'secret chamber', a kind of board room, full of dark benches; there are Byzantine crucifixes, fairly horrible, and a painting of St Bartholomew being, as the guide puts it, 'skinned alive'. When I turn away in disgust he apologizes.

It is a relief to descend into the square and cross it to the small garden which gives access to the fortification called the Rocca, now only a ruin, but a fine viewpoint, with the towers in the foreground and the valley below, with the Apennines lost in mist in the distance. The garden gate is unlocked by an unsmiling woman who emerges from a small cottage hidden among vines at one side. The guide marches ahead up the steep rough steps which are really only boulders.

All that is left of the Rocca, the castle, which was begun in 1353, is the ruined surviving tower, and it seems wrong to charge an admission fee simply for the view out over the valley and a close-up of five of San Gimignano's thirteen remaining towers. 'Beautiful view,' says the guide, and waits, sombrely, for me have done with it. A lizard slides along the warm sunny wall and disappears into some bushes. There are birds in tiny cages hung on the walls of houses down below. There is an endless cawing of crows above the gaunt grey towers. We are joined by a young German couple, animated, eager, the young man with his camera at the ready. I turn away and follow the guide down over the boulders.

I would like, now, to return to the friendly Angelino, but there is another church on the routine itinerary, Sant' Agostino, the church of St Augustine. It is late thirteenth century, and small, which, after all the grandiose churches, makes a nice change. There are frescoes, of course; frescoes galore, covering the walls, and they, equally of course, include a series depicting the life of St Augustine; one of them shows him with his mother St Monica and his child.

Many years ago I was very interested in Augustine of Hippo, and I am interested now, as I gaze at the fifteenth-century frescoes, but there has been a surfeit of frescoes, and exhaustion is creeping up on me and I cannot take in any more. There are cloisters, with cypresses and a palm or two, and the inevitable well, and some Etruscan relics.

Angelino waits with the car in the piazza. The guide says, simply, 'Finished!', bows slightly, unsmiling, turns abruptly and strides off, hands still clasped behind his back, head down.

'Now!' says Angelino, cheerfully, 'Siena!'

10

SOMETHING OF
SIENA

DRIVING through the endless vineyards from San Gimignano to
Siena, via the attractive old town of Colle Val d'Elsa, and wearying
of grapes, grapes all the way, I thought about the whole business of
guides. It is no reflection on the professional capabilities of the guide
at San Gimignano when I say that I believe that on my own I
would have absorbed more of the atmosphere of the place – and
liked it better. I don't think I know any more about the cathedral by
having been officially 'shown' it; I would hardly have missed it – the
cathedral is invariably the first objective in any city anywhere. I
might have missed the Rocca – but the view is available anyhow,
without toiling up there; I might have skipped the museum, not
being very fond of museums; but I would have mooched – and
there is nothing like mooching in a strange town or city for getting
the 'feel' of it.

If the San Gimignano guide had been more *simpatico* as a per-
sonality, I still think I would have done better on my own. Assisi
had been different: seeing it with the very nice Englishwoman had
been like being shown around by a friend who knew the place,
and the conducted tour had been both pleasant and helpful. Given
an impersonal guide I'd have been better on my own. Official guides
were a new experience for me. In my Middle East travels I was
provided with 'escorts' by the various Arab ministries of information
whose guest I was; that was something different; they were provided because I do not, unfortunately, speak Arabic; they were not
'official'; they were simply part of the hospitality. I was not, in any
case, 'touring' any of the Arab countries; but there were certain

things they wanted me to see – industrial and agricultural projects, schools, housing-schemes – and certain things I wanted to see – Petra, in Jordan, Palmyra in Syria, Ur of the Chaldees in Iraq (and Nineveh and Babylon and Samarra), the island of Failaka, off Kuwait – and to go alone to such places would have been difficult if not impossible; so that I had to have 'escorts'. But all that is something quite different from the official guide, to whom it is all routine, whether it is a group or an individual. In Japan, in 1959, I travelled extensively, by train, second-class, and alone, and visited many towns and villages and pagodas, without benefit of guides. The guide on the villas tour outside Venice was good, and he was also, really, essential. The guide for the mosaics at Ravenna was useless, as I have recounted. The little guide on the coach from Venice to Florence was definitely helpful, pointing out things along the route which we should otherwise have missed.

Anyhow, there we were, Angelino and I, speeding through the vineyard country from San Gimignano to Siena, and there another guide awaited me for my brief visit, and if he marched me about as silently and gloomily as the one from whom I had just parted I should break down and *cry*, I thought, as we drove through the vineyards to Colle Val d'Elsa with its steep narrow streets. There are wild birds in small cages along a wall – a long row of them – reflecting the cruelty that spoils life. We descend to the modern part of the town, and a narrow river. We drive out of the town into ploughed land with red earth, and vineyards, and men and women cutting the bunches of grapes in the warm sunshine. We pass a hill-top village like San Gimignano, with walls and towers – 'the *avant-garde* for Siena', says Angelino.

There are advertisement hoardings along the lovely wooded road, and the first sight of Siena is an ugly huddle of blocks of flats. Why, I wonder, are the outskirts of even the most beautiful cities, invariably so hideous?

'No industry in Siena,' says Angelino, 'only tourism and banking.'

We enter the city, where the buildings are all of that lovely reddish-brown colour described in our school paint boxes as 'burnt Siena'.

Angelino parks the car opposite the great Excelsior Hotel, with the small public gardens of La Lizza behind. He conducts me across the road to a café where I may have my lunchtime Campari and a sandwich and wash my hands – he is ever solicitous about that important function. The guide is to arrive at 2.20, and he knows where to find us; it is now one o'clock. Angelino settles me and leaves me. I sit at a table on the café terrace with the Campari-soda and sandwich he has ordered for me, but the sun is too warm to linger here, and I move off and find a shop where they sell ice-cream, and when I have furnished myself with a great dollop of ice-cream perched on a cornet I continue to mooch. I precariously cross several roads whizzing with cars and get back to the Excelsior, and wander in La Lizza, pleasant with tall trees and avenues and grass, and views out over the city. There is a statue of Garibaldi, and a café with chairs and tables set out under trees and a sound of music.

I get back to the car soon after two, and Angelino and I sit and wait. When no guide has turned up by 2.45 Angelino becomes worried and goes off to a call-box to telephone the guide's house. He returns to say that he has spoken to the signora and she says her husband has just left. A few minutes later he arrives, leisurely, a short, thickset figure, wearing dark glasses.

'I am punctual,' he astonishingly announces.

Angelino protests that we expected him nearly half an hour ago and that he has just telephoned his house.

Imperturbably he replies, 'Family lunches sometimes take a long time.'

He regards me through the dark glasses and declares, 'I am like a tailor. Before I can make you a suit I must take your measure.'

I dislike, quite intensely, being stared at through dark glasses, because whereas the wearer can see out you cannot see in, and unless you can see a person's eyes any conversation is 'blind'.

My hackles rose, and I said, a little sharply, 'I merely want to see whatever you can show me this afternoon.'

His smile was ironic.

'What do you expect to see in a few hours?'

'There should be time for a few things.'

'Why do you not stay for several days?'

'It has been arranged for me to go to Verona tomorrow.'

'How long do you stay in Verona?'

'Three days.'

'Three days in Verona! And you come to Siena for three hours!' He all but spat.

I did not feel inclined to be driven into the defensive position of explaining that I had not planned the itinerary myself, or that I had not realized that Siena was so important – both of which were true – and I merely said, coldy, 'There is time to visit the cathedral.'

Angelino quickly followed up the cue.

'I cannot stay here with the car. Let us drive to the Duomo.'

We got into the car and this time I sat at the back, waving away Angelino's tentative protest.

We drove to the Piazza del Duomo, through streets wide and narrow, and the first sight of the cathedral I found almost as staggering in its beauty as the first sight of St Mark's in Venice. The façade is delicately ornate, of polychromatic marble; there are three gables of mosaics, the two lower ones supported by columns; there is a tall campanile, also banded in black and white marble; there are columns surmounted by the she-wolf of Siena suckling Romulus and Remus. I felt that I would have liked to have come to it alone, to be able to stand and stare, as when I had first been confronted by St Mark's.

Angelino parked the car and the guide and I got out, and we did not, to my surprise, ascend the marble steps of the cathedral; instead we walked. Of that I was glad; I am of that almost extinct species of the human race that likes to walk, and for the purpose of getting to know a place regards it as essential. Also, walking the guide and

I might get to know each other as human beings – not just as
guide and tourist. He might, even, remove his dark glasses.

He did, though I have fogotten at what point. We walked and we
talked. He showed me a house with a flag outside, and blue ribbons
– a registrar's office, I think – to denote the birth of a boy in the
district, that day. He explained that this was the 'dragon district',
and that Siena was divided into wards, seventeen *contrade*, each
with the name of a bird or beast. We came into the district of the
owl. There was the Roman she-wolf, on a pedestal – Siena began as
Saena Julia, a Roman colony founded by Augustus.

We come to the Piazza Tolomei, on which stands the Palazzo
Tolomei, thirteenth century and the oldest private Gothic palace
in Siena. Siena, like Vienna, is full of palaces, and they are all
handsome. This is the banking area, and I am taken into a bank
which outside is like a palace and inside like a cathedral, with brick
pillars and a vaulted brick ceiling. It is thirteenth century, and in
the middle of it there is a deep well, a 'cistern', with a spiral staircase down. But in all other respects it is a bank like any other,
with young men and girls busy behind counters and at desks.

At some point, as we stroll in a narrow street which looks down
into the lane in which there is the Casa di Santa Caterina, the house
of St Catherine of Siena, I stop to look in at the window of a wine
shop, my attention attracted by bottles of Chianti – I had hitherto
seen this wine only in the wicker-covered flasks. It is explained to
me that the best Chianti is labelled Classico, and there is the emblem
of a black cock on the neck of the bottle. 'You are interested in
wine?'

I say, well, yes –

He tells me this and that about Italian wines as we walk on and
then pauses outside a house which looks to me like a small palace,
but it is a restaurant now, whatever it may have been in the past, and
he wishes to show it to me.

It is certainly worthy of inspection, for the beautiful vaulted ceiling of the interior, and its pale, cool elegance. The middle-aged
woman seated at the cash desk near the entrance rises all smiles

and greetings; she and the guide are evidently old friends. What he says to her I do not know, since it is spoken in Italian, but she leads us to a pillar in the middle of the room, where on a kind of bar which encircles the pillar there are many bottles and a tall vase of gladioli. She pours from one of the bottles and hands each of us a glass. It is some kind of vermouth, bitter-sweet, very strong, very good. We sip it and it glows pleasantly in the veins. When we shake hands with the signora and leave the restaurant we are somehow on much matier terms than when we entered; we are laughing, and at one point a hand is laid playfully on an arm. In this new matiness he tells me that Paul Bourget, 'the French poet' (but he was primarily a novelist), said that 'Rome was for the religious, Venice for lovers, Florence for tourists, but Siena was reserved for only a few connoisseurs.'

Whether Paul Bourget said anything of the kind I have no idea, but I was commanded to 'write it down', so I wrote it down, and was admitted, it seemed, into the honourable order of the few.

We are now on the way to the Duomo, and we come first to the little chapel, the Baptistery of St John, and I did not understand at the time that this is the crypt of the cathedral. I did not understand this because it was not explained to me, and also because you enter the Baptistery off the Piazza San Giovanni, behind the cathedral, and unless you have had it explained to you there is no reason at all to suppose it is other than a small church; but when you are in the cathedral you can look through a grille by the high altar down into the Baptistery. It seems puzzling, but is all to do with the different ground levels on which the cathedral has been built.

Anyhow, we entered from the piazza, and for those who like such architectural particulars the Official Guide records that the façade of the Baptistery of St John is 'sober', and 'articulated by three deep portals, corresponding with three gothic windows above an elegant gallery of little arches', and 'exquisite harmony is achieved by the use of polychrome marbles and delightful decorative motives'.

The description continues: 'The interior of the Baptistery presents a magnificent scheme of decoration consisting of frescoes adorning the vault and the walls. The famous baptismal font dominates in the centre; it is a polygonal bowl adorned with bronze reliefs made by Ghiberti, Donatello, Jacopo della Quercia and Giovanni di Turino. The marble tabernacle is a late work by Jacopo della Quercia.'

I have seen a coloured photograph bearing out this decription: it looks wonderful. But all I remember is the font; my recollection is of being taken in and immediately confronted by the font, which I was told was the combined work of Donatello, Ghiberti, and Quercia who united to create 'this beautiful baptismal fountain'.

The interior of the cathedral, which is dedicated to the Assumption, is staggering. It is all black and white striped marble, with enormous pillars, and seemed to me more like a mosque than a church – even the campanile is like a minaret. The marble floor, the pavement, or 'piazza', is like a great carpet in a mosque; you do not have to remove your shoes to walk on it, but in places, where it is especially precious, it is covered over. The patterns in the floor depict biblical and allegorical scenes, and are the work of forty-five Sienese artists of the fourteenth and sixteenth centuries.

There is a seventeenth-century baroque chapel, the Capella Chigi, with statues by Bernini, with wonderful lapis-lazuli mosaics and above the altar a most beautiful painting of Our Lady of Siena attributed to Guido da Siena – a thirteenth-century work, and much venerated by the Sienese. Prayers for deliverance have several times in the course of history been offered up before it, the last occasion being on June 18, 1944, a fortnight before the liberation of Siena. I liked this chapel very much indeed.

The supreme feature of the cathedral is the thirteenth-century octagonal marble pulpit carved by Nicola Pisano, who, my friend the guide insisted, was the first to 'humanize' Christ – not Giotto. Nicola Pisano was twenty years before Giotto. But how could I see this masterpiece, the basis of the culture of Europe, the starting point of the Renaissance – 'which is why it is so important' – in a few minutes? 'It would take me two hours to explain it to you!' He sank down on to a stone bench facing the masterpiece. 'Sit here beside me,' he commanded. I obeyed, and attempted to assuage that anguish of despair. 'I can read it all up when I get back,' I said, soothingly.

'When you get back! But you are here now, and it is here you should understand it! It took six people three years to create it! There are four hundred and eighty figures in the carving!'

Figures like that convey nothing, of course, The pulpit is enormous; marble pillars support the elaborate carving at the top, and there are lions at the base; the seven relief panels of the parapet depict scenes from the life of Christ.

I gazed respectfully and murmured that it was very beautiful – wonderful –

I really did think this, but I also thought that to spend two hours on it would be too much – anyhow for a cultural ignoramus such as myself. But it was pleasant to sit for a few minutes after so much walking and standing about.

On the way to the library, opening off the north aisle, there was the diversion of a young woman suddenly detaching herself from the tall young man who was with her, rushing over to my companion, crying his name, and literally hurling herself upon him in wild embraces. He responded by flinging his arms about her, and there was a great exchange of kissing on both cheeks, and of glad cries. The young man and I stood back, tactfully, politely. I think we both thought that in a moment there would be an exchange of introductions; I certainly did. When none was forthcoming the young man wandered away, and I went on into the library, with its statues of the Three Graces and its brightly coloured frescoes, fifteenth century and depicting scenes from the life of Pope Pius II.

I was duly joined there by my-friend-the-guide, as he seemed somehow to have become, and I expected that he would explain to me that the young woman was a beloved long-lost niece, or a younger sister, but it seemed she was an English girl to whom a few years ago he had taught Italian at the university's language school for foreigners. 'Then,' he said, 'she was a sweet and nice and pretty

Perugia, exterior of the Rocco Paolina: 'the roofed-over walled city within
the walled city of Perugia.'

Perugia, street scene: 'the city was founded by the Etruscans, whose walls
still stand.'

Perugia, interior of the Rocca Paolina: '... streets going off into darkness ...
Like a stage set, unreal, but sinister.'

girl. Now, as you can see, she is a lovely young woman! The young man is her fiancé. He is to be much congratulated.'

He sighed, and turned a lustreless gaze on the supernaturally bright frescoes.

'She seems very fond of you,' I comforted him.

He brightened then. Yes, he agreed, and added, happily, 'Everyone likes Giuseppe.'

(That is not his name, but it will serve.)

We resumed attention on to the frescoes.

'Heavily restored?' I suggested.

He declared emphatically that they were not. The frescoes are early sixteenth century; they are by Pinturicchio and his pupils, and one depicts Pius II canonizing Catherine of Siena. Massive vellum choir books of the cathedral are displayed on massive carved benches below the frescoes. You gaze respectfully. What else can you do?

We emerge again into the cathedral, and I am shown a huge lectern with an enormous bible thereon, and am told that the cathedral is sometimes used for concerts at which are played the works of Bach and Vivaldi, amongst others, and *Parsifal* has been given there.

From the cathedral it is no distance along the Via dei Pellegrini to the Piazza del Campo, the city's main square, which is of very great beauty, and very remarkable, being a shallow fan-shaped bowl, flanked by lovely red brick old houses and palaces, and dominated by the battlemented, Gothic Palazzo Pubblico, late thirteenth, early fourteenth century, and the great red-brown Mangia tower, which is for me much more the symbol of Siena than the Roman she-wolf . . . though this somewhat obscene beast is everywhere, even at the Campo.

The Campo, occupying the site of the Roman forum, is the scene of the celebrated horse races, the Palio, held in July and August, and for which each *contrada* enters a horse, and the winning ward gives a banquet, in which the horse shares, eating from its own manger. The Palio is held with full medieval pageantry, the jockeys

G

splendid in black and scarlet velvet, and before the race there is a spectacular parade, with flag-throwing, and a triumphal chariot drawn by four white oxen – all somewhat reminiscent, it would seem, of the parade which precedes a Spanish bullfight. But during the Palio no one is killed or injured, and the race is for the *palio*, or banner, and the honour of the victory goes not to any individual but to the *contrada*. Strangely, the *fantini*, or jockeys, whip not only their own horses along but those of their competitors. The races go back to the seventeenth century; they are held on the feast of the Visitation, July 2, and of the Assumption, August 16. During the Palio, I was told, the hotels are heavily booked and the prices go up. I was shown a book, at a bookstall beside the Campo, with coloured pictures of the Palio. That it was tremendously exciting and richly spectacular I felt sure, but I was by then too tired to take any more in.

To the end the attempt was made to induce me to stay overnight for another day's exploration of the city.

'What can you write for your book after a visit of only a few hours?' he demanded.

This, of course, was second-time-round. Where I had come in.

I said, evenly, that I had seen quite a lot, and it would make a chapter. One day it might be possible to return and see more, but now I was commited to returning to Florence and continuing on to Verona tomorrow; otherwise my whole itinerary was thrown out. I had to work to schedule.

I held out my hand.

'Thank you,' I said. 'You have shown me a great deal. I am very grateful.'

He took my hand in a strong grip.

'It is a pity,' he said.

'Yes. But with any luck I'll be back. For now it's good-bye – and thank you again.'

'It was a pleasure,' he assured me, and I had the feeling that he really meant it; that we had somehow achieved a mutual respect.

'*Arrivederci*,' he said.

Angelino waited patiently, detachedly, beside the car. I got in; there was a small final wave, then we headed out across the lovely red brick city glowing in the mellow evening sunlight. We made our exit through triple gates in the ancient walls, passed the handsome red brick railway station, with its gay flower-beds in front, and were soon out on the motorway, heading for Florence at a hundred kilometres an hour.

'This way, the *autostrada*, it is quicker,' said Angelino.

II
VERONA: 'VENICE
WITHOUT THE WATER'

By Alpes Express from Florence to Verona sounds romantic, but is, in fact, a singularly dull train journey – anyhow after Bologna, where you leave the Apennines and cross the featureless Lombardy plain, with agricultural lands at either side the line all the way. But the first sight of Verona is exciting, with green hills rising above it and one crowned by a round building, white and classical.

Verona is, simply, a very beautiful city. Almost every building in it, almost every house, is beautiful. Much as I regretted having had only three hours in the wonderful city of Siena, if it came to the choice of three hours in Siena versus three days in Verona I would still settle for the three days in Verona. It is not enough; Verona demands a minimum of five days. Nevertheless, in three days, on my own, blessedly free of guides, I saw a great deal, and got the 'feel' of the city. I didn't get to Lake Garda, but I don't think I missed anything 'essential'. Verona has been called the 'Gateway to Italy', and 'Venice without the water' and second only to Venice for the interest of its monuments. It is a tragedy that because it is Venice-without-the-water, and has roads instead of canals, it should be so heavily polluted by traffic, of a density even more horrific than in Florence. When you climb to the top of the tremendous Roman amphitheatre and look down on the Piazza Brà, which is the city's biggest square, and very beautiful, with gardens and cedars and fountains, the traffic circling endlessly around is like a black, close-packed line of ants.

Exploration of Verona begins, naturally, I think, with the Piazza Brà, as in London it would begin, I would think, with Trafalgar

Square, and in Paris with the Place de la Concorde, and in Venice, of course, with the Piazza San Marco. The Piazza Brà is flanked at one side by the Arena, which is like the Colosseum in Rome, and across the gardens, with their cedars, by the broad pavement lined with cafés known as the 'Listone', a popular promenade. In the middle of the gardens there is an equestrian statue of Vittorio Emmanuel II. The other sides of the square are flanked by palaces which according to the official guide are of 'great architectural importance', and undoubtedly they are, but I will content myself by saying, simply, that they are very handsome buildings, one of them seventeenth century, the others later. There is a great gateway of two huge arches, the Portoni della Brà, with battlements, part of the fourteenth-century Visconti walls, and there is a great tower, and there are arcades, and it is all very beautiful and splendid and exciting.

If you wander around behind the amphitheatre you come to the Via Mazzini, which is, blessedly, a pedestrian thoroughfare, but very crowded. According to the Official Guide it is the only pedestrian thoroughfare in the city, but though this may have been true in 1971, the date of the guide, in 1973, when I was there, the Via Cappello, crossing the Via Mazzini and the Via della Stella, was also pedestrian. There is a whole labyrinth of narrow streets here, and in spite of a street map I was continually lost, and I came upon Juliet's House, in a courtyard, off the Via Cappello, entirely by accident. The Casa di Guilietta is a very beautiful brick-built thirteenth-century house with, of course, a balcony, stone-carved, and romantic. On the wall of the house there is a plaque with a quotation from the balcony scene. There is a charming little bronze statue of Juliet, and along the walls of the building opposite the Casa di Guilietta there are devices – ear-phones – by means of which visitors may listen to an account of the Romeo and Juliet story in English, French, Italian, German, as required – instant culture. According to the Blue Guide the house was once an inn with the sign 'Il Cappello', identifying it with the Capulet family to which Juliet belonged. (But it is no longer correct that as the Blue Guide states the city tourist office is installed in 'the so-called Casa di Guilietta'. This is now behind the 'Listone', the popular, café-flanked promenade on the Piazza Brà, and singularly unhelpful I found it.)

Round the corner from here, through the Arche Scaligeri, is the Piazza delle Erbe, on the site of the Roman forum. It is a market square, flanked by handsome buildings, most of them palaces, and though I would not agree with the Official Guide that it is 'the most beautiful spot in Verona', I found it completely facinating, liking market places as I do, and this one, with its tall square tower, and its lovely frescoed house-fronts, and its palaces, being something quite special in market squares. The pavement of the square is almost roofed-over by a mass of huge, flat umbrellas extended over stalls of all kinds – fruit, vegetables, pottery, toys, cakes and sweets, secondhand books and paperbacks, clothes, and, alas, little brightly-plumaged birds in tiny cages . . . a sorrowful sight to be seen all over Italy.

In the middle of the square there is a fourteenth-century fountain, with a Roman statue, the Madonna Verona, and there are cafés, and a column supporting a Venetian lion – it is called the Colonna di San Marco. (For those who like historical particulars – after the fall of the house of Scaliger, the ruling family, Visconti, became 'tyrant of the city', but in 1405 Verona placed itself under the aegis of St Mark.)

Through another arch, the Arco della Costa, you come to the distinguished Piazza dei Signori, with its monument to Dante in the middle, the monument is nineteenth century, perched high on a pedestal, unremarkable, but much patronized by pigeons and by camera-clicking tourists. There is a Café Dante in the eighteenth-century Domus Nova; the café still maintains its original nineteenth-century décor.

Just as Napoleon called the Piazza San Marco the drawing-room of Europe, the Piazza dei Signori has been called the drawing-room of Verona. Certainly it is very elegant, with its handsome palaces, their façades of alternating bands of red brick and stonework its Loggia del Consiglio, with its lovely arches, and said to be the most outstanding of all the Renaissance buildings in Verona, and the beautiful, stately red-brick Palazzo del Scaligeri, now the Prefettura. A café, with tables and chairs out in the piazza, looks directly across to the palace of the Scala family, with the wonderful Loggia on the left.

Tucked away in a corner, behind the palace, there is the dark, ancient little church of Santa Maria Antica, dating from the seventh century. It is considered to be a fine example of early Romanesque architecture; I remember only the smallness and darkness, stone arches, and innumerable candles. Over a porch at the side of the church is the sarcophagus of Cangrande I della Scala, who died in 1329. He ruled the city for eighteen years, and during his reign Verona is said to have reached the peak of its magnificence. In this corner, by the little church, there are two ornate erections oddly reminiscent of the Albert Memorial in London; they stand in an enclosure of beautiful wrought-iron railings bearing the emblems of the Scala family and surmounted by statues of angels. Admission 100 lire – though how much more is to be seen by entering the enclosure I really don't know, for it seemed to me that everything could be seen very well by walking round outside and peering through. Anyhow, this architectural complex is the Arche Scaligeri and contains the tombs of the Scala family. At the top of the central spire of the nearest monument there is a statue of Cangrande on horseback, the work of an anonymous sculptor of the fourteenth century, and considered a masterpiece. According to the Official Guide 'the Scala family monuments represent the pinnacle reached by Gothic art in Verona'.

Through the archway, in the Via della Arche Scaligeri, the dilapidated Gothic house at the corner is Romeo's house. It is of dark brick, and its windows, with shabby shutters, from which the grey paint is peeling, suggests a decaying tenement housing seedy apartments. It has a general air of dereliction of a once great house come down in the world; a long way down. The Official Guide describes it as a 'fine medieval building popularly identified with the house of the Montecchi or Montagues, Romeo's family', but admits that it is in such bad condition that no visitors are admitted. There is a plaque with a quotation from the play.

Across from Romeo's house is the Piazza Independenza, with cedars and shrubs, and grass and flowers, and an equestrian statue of Garibaldi. This is an unimportant square, and shabby, like Romeo's house on the corner, but it is quiet, and there are seats. and it is another refuge from the traffic. I rested a little on a seat, made up some notes, watched pigeons and children going about their intensely personal business, consulted the map, then continued in the direction of the river, with the Duomo as my objective. This is not the most direct route to the Duomo from that point, but I yearned for the river.

(It should perhaps be explained at this point that when you are in the Piazza Brà, or the Piazza Erbe, that is to say the city centre, you have the River Adige at either side. From the Piazza Erbe you can walk westward to the Ponte Vittoria, or eastward to the Ponte Nuovo. Walking from the Piazza Independenza along the Via Ponte Pietra I was heading for the bridge at the head of the peninsula looped by the river, with the Duomo a little to the west of it.)

The direct route to the Duomo would have been along the Via Duomo; I made a détour along the Via Ponte Pietra to the river. There were beautiful decaying old houses – one with faded murals, another like a small palace with Gothic windows – very Venetian it seemed to me, though, of course, what it is is very Veronese. Then under an arch and on to the bridge, for the view up and down the fast-flowing river, and the Castle of St Peter at the other side, high on the green hillside, with the Roman theatre among its cypresses below it. It is a very fine view, one of many along this rushing rapid of a river.

I did not, then, cross the bridge, being concerned with the Duomo, the twelfth-century cathedral of Santa Maria Matricolare. It stands in a small square, flanked by old houses, and is a mixture of Romanesque and Gothic, with little spires rising everywhere, like turrets, and two porches, one above the other, the upper one with a clock. The façade is a mixture of brick and stone and marble – it has been described as 'architecture in colour'. To me it looked a mess and I cannot report much on the interior because it was too dark to make out anything but lofty pillars fanning out at the top like great stone trees. Important to make out, once your eyes become accustomed to the gloom, is the dark painting above the altar in the first chapel in the north aisle; it is Titian's Assumption of the Virgin Mary, the only work he executed in Verona.

Across an ugly iron bridge to some ugly modern blocks of flats – can this still be Verona? – and along the Lungadige San Giorgio, as streaming with cars as the embankment of the Seine in Paris, to the domed church of San Giorgio in Braida, which had interested me from the other side of the river. The church is fifteenth century and reached through some public gardens. As it was midday I could not get in, which was a relief, truth to tell, but inside there are some Tintorettos, and the church is considered to be one of the richest in works of art in Verona.

I continued on along the embankment and recrossed the river at the Ponte Pietra, and after the traffic at the other side it was a relief to be again in the relatively quiet streets of old houses that lead back to the Piazza Erbe and the labyrinth of lanes beyond, where, in the Via Mazzini, you can hear, blessedly the sound of footsteps and voices, as in Venice.

In the afternoon I walked again in the direction of the river, but this time southward along the Via degli Alpini and the Visconti walls to the Via Palloni and the Ponte Aleardi, which looks across the river to an avenue of cypresses leading to the huge monument of the Cimitero, surmounted by angels, and writ large across it the word *Ressurecturis*. There is a fine view along the river to St Peter's Castle, but the traffic pouring across the bridge, and along the embankment at the other side, is a nightmare. I thought, as I had in Florence, that if many more cars and scooters go on to the Italian roads they will be choked to a standstill. The zebra crossings are not treated with the respect with which they are treated in England and are of little help to pedestrians; there are a few subways; elsewhere you cross the roads at your peril, and the preponderance of scooters add to the nightmare, since the aim of every Italian scooter-rider seems to be to travel at maximum speed, with the maximum noise.

The Via Roma is a noisy commercial street leading westward from the Piazza Brà to the fantastic Ponte Scaligero, which leads from the equally fantastic Castelvecchio, now the City Museum, across to the gardens of the Piazza Arsenale, with tall trees, and fountains, and seats, and the collegiate-looking building of the arsenal beyond. It is a relief to leave the Via Roma and pass in under an arch to the lovely garden in front of the museum. There are fountains and flowers, and goldfish glide in shallow pools, and little lizards dart along the sun-warmed stone of low parapets. All round are the ancient walls and keeps of the castle, muting the scream of scooters along the Corso Cavour.

The Castelvecchio was built for Cangrande II in 1354 as a citadel. It is fantastic because it is so massive, so crenellated, so lavish with towers and ramparts and courtyards, so exaggeratedly medieval, and as if that wasn't enough there is the fabulous Ponte Scaligero leading on from it, with still more heavily crenellated walls and keeps.

The castle became barracks in the late eighteenth century, under the French, Austrians, Italians, until 1923. In 1925 it was inaugurated as a museum by Vittorio Emmanuel III. It was damaged during World War II, and restored, and the museum re-created by Carlo Scarpa in 1956–64. According to the Official Guide it is 'now considered one of the best-laid-out museums in the whole of Europe'. That is something upon which I could have no opinion, but crossing the drawbridge and the courtyard, and entering the Napoleonic east wing, I was very impressed, because it is not like being in a museum or a picture gallery but is always a medieval castle – in which there are splendid sculptures and paintings . . . and a very fine view of the bridge. There are stone stairs and covered passages connecting walls and keeps, and at one point an astonishing equestrian state of Cangrande high on a plinth below a crenellated wall, brought from the cemetery of the Scala family. It is curiously Don Quixotish, with the horse draped, fore and aft, and Cangrande carrying what would appear to be his helmet over his shoulder. To my simple mind it was grotesque and comical, and I bought a postcard of it to send to my young grand-daughter, who likes horses.

You continue on and up and pass through the fortress wall and come to the main keep, and after room VII, with massive fourteenth-century bells, stairs lead up to a room with weaponry, and a bridge leads across to a room full of frescoes. Then in room XII there are some Bellinis, and the most beautiful Madonna of the Quail, by Pisanello. In this painting the Madonna is very young, and golden-haired, and leaning towards the golden Child the curve of her head and neck is one with the flow of her dark robe; above there is a curve of two angels with blue wings.

Beautiful, also, in this room is Stefano de Verona's formal Madonna of the Rosebower, with a dark-robed Madonna – also golden-haired – against a kind of tapestry of roses and foliage. Into this tapestry are woven blue-winged angels.

In room XVI there are Mantegnas, outstandingly a wonderful painting of Christ carrying the Cross, in which the exhaustion and suffering is most poignantly depicted.

In room XXII I was impressed by a Caroto painting of a young Benedictine monk, the boy's serious face one of great spirituality. In Room XXVI there are Marcantonio Bassetti portraits, and there is what was for me a profoundly moving portrait of St Anthony of Padua. I was moved by what I can only define as the spiritual beauty expressed in this painting. There are, alas, no postcards of it, nor is it, that I could see, reproduced in any of the books about the paintings in the museum. The saint is shown in the dark brown Capucine habit, the cowl pushed back from the forehead, and reading a book open on the table at which he sits. The face is thoughtful, intelligent, spiritual . . . which adds up to something very beautiful. The right hand rests against the face; the left hand holds the open book; a madonna lily lies across the table. The young man who was to become St Anthony of Padua, and whose baptismal name was Fernandez, was born in Lisbon in 1195, and joined the Franciscans in 1220, that is to say when he was twenty-five. He died near Padua in 1231, at the age of thirty-six. In 1221 Francis of Assisi made him the order's first lector of theology, and as such he taught at Bologna, Montpellier and Toulouse.

These are the paintings which impressed and moved me, and of which I made notes. For the rest, passing from room to room, there seemed too many crucifixions, descents from the cross, annunciations, assumptions, Madonnas-and-Child. If you have been in both Venice and Florence saturation point on all this, in churches and art galleries, is reached long before Verona.

When I left the castle I walked along the walled, cobbled 'street' which is the interior of the bridge, though as you walk along it is difficult to realize that it is a bridge. It is barred to traffic. The bridge was built for Cangrande a year after the castle. It was almost totally destroyed in World War II, but has been faithfully reconstructed, like the Ponte Pietra, which was similarly destroyed.

Returning to the Castelvecchio I walked out along the river to San Zeno Maggiore, considered one of the most beautiful Romanesque churches in northern Italy, dating from the twelfth century and completed in the thirteenth.

This walk along the Regaste, under acacia trees, with the road below, is very pleasant, and, with the patrician old houses, reminded me of the Île St Louis, Paris. There are benches under the trees, and a cooling wind along the river – the day was warm – and though the traffic hurtles along the road below there is nevertheless the blessed feeling of having escaped from it, and though at this part of the river you no longer have the lovely sight of the Castle of St Peter, red brick, crenellated, and sentinelled by cypresses, on its hill, you have, looking back, the red brick of the arches and towers of the fantastic Ponte Scaligero. Of all the things I did in Verona I most enjoyed this walk along the Regaste San Zeno.

I recorded in my on-the-spot notes that the area around the church was 'like coming to another town. A lovely square with trees and

seats.' The paved square in front of the church is huge, and dominated by the great campanile, dating from the first half of the twelfth
century, and is considered a superb example of its period. At the
other side of the church there is a square tower, red brick and crenellated, also twelfth century, and the remains of an ancient monastery – 'mentioned by Dante in Canto 18 of his Purgatory'.

The great bronze doors constitute the main feature of the exterior
of the church; they depict scenes from the Old and New Testaments
of the Bible, and the Miracles of San Zeno, and if you intend to
examine them in detail you will be there all day. But the general
effect is handsome. For those who want the details it's all in the
Official Guide – illustrated. According to the Guide they 'undoubtedly possess great primitive power, reminiscent of the style
of icons'.

As the reader will by now have gathered I always dread important churches, feeling unable to cope; but I needn't have dreaded
the interior of the Basilica of San Zeno Maggiore because it is
simply beautiful, and the key-word is simply. There are grey pillars
and columns and a remarkable Gothic wooden roof. Across a wide
'piazza' you descend to the lower church, or crypt, and here there
is the tomb of St Zeno; the Official Guide describes it as an urn; it
is in fact a glass case in which the bishop lies in his red robes, and
whether this is another of those 'incorruptible' bodies I do not know,
and I do but report. Neither the Official Guide nor the Blue Guide
have anything to say on the matter; the latter merely reports 'the
tomb of St Zeno, 1889'. The Official Guide refers to 'the urn
holding the body of St Zeno'. The glass case is lighted from within,
and the bishop is anyhow not black in the face. There are a great
many pillars in the crypt, with candelabra suspended between, and
unlike most crypts, which tend to be creepy, it is a cheerful cave-of-
Aladdin kind of place.

In the upper church, amongst the cool and grey, there are faded
frescoes, and above the high altar a triptych by Mantegna, a Madonna and Child, with Saints, a complicated work with many figures,
and considered a masterpiece of the Venetian Renaissance, but

pas pour moi. The cloisters, grassy, with columns, spoke more to my condition.

But undoubtedly this is a very beautiful church, not florid as Italian churches so commonly are, and it is a lovely walk to it along the river, under the shady acacias.

In the afternoon, after careful studying of the map, I plotted a course to the Giusti Gardens, via the Piazza Erbe and the Piazza Independenza, crossing the river by the Ponte Nuovo. At the other side you follow the Via Muro Padri, which leads on to the Via Gusti, where, at Number 2, is the somewhat hidden entrance to the gardens under an archway through the buildings. An official emerges from an office in the archway, there being a small admission charge, and instead of a ticket you are given a coloured picture postcard of the gardens.

In general I am not much attracted to formal gardens, but in Italian cities gardens of any kind are precious havens from the roar and shriek and clangour of the streets. Also, if you are a visitor, they make a change from churches. The Giusti Gardens are sixteenth century, and were designed for the Palazzo Giusti. The Blue Guide describes them as a 'magnificent hillside pleasance', and certainly they are very beautiful, laid out with flower beds with box borders, and stately with statuary and fountains. There are also some remarkably fine trees – spreading cedars and tall, splendid cypresses – and cobbled paths climb up, with occasional flights of rough steps, through wooded slopes to a belvedere, with a fine view out over the city's red roofs, towers, campaniles. There is a tower with a spirial staircase and a platform at the top for a higher view, but on a warm day it seemed not worth the effort. The small church of San Zeno in Monte is at the top of the wooded slopes, surrounded by cypresses; it has the distinction of having been very much admired by Goethe.

I was joined at the belvedere by an Italian family party; I left them there, after a polite exchange of greetings, and, descending, saw no other visitors.

Returning across the Ponte Nuovo to the Piazza Erbe it was pleasant to sit at a small café with a Campari-soda before continuing on to lose myself – as I invariably did – in the labyrinth of narrow streets at the other side in my search for the eighteenth-century palazzo in the Via Mazzini which is now the Hotel Accademia, just round the corner from Juliet's house. I was always making notes in aid of myself: 'Returning from Piazza Erbe turn right into the Via Stella. Perfume shop on corner. Frette clothing store opposite.' But still I got lost, and was perpetually accosting Veronese citizens; fortunately Italians everywhere, I found, are very good-natured in dealing with lost visitors who first inquire the way, with the preliminary *scusi*, and then, having only half a dozen words of Italian, fail to understand the instructions so carefully given them, though they continue on their way with smiles and thanks and pretences of comprehension.

There remained, for my last day in Verona, the great Roman amphitheatre, the Arena, at the city's heart, and its most important monument.

A small square opposite the Arena is the Piazza Gallienus, with the remains of Roman walls. According to the Official Guide the amphitheatre was originally outside the city walls, but in the third century the Emperor Gallienus extended the walls, as a defensive measure, enclosing the amphitheatre within them. The amphitheatre is believed to have been built two hundred years earlier. It is the third largest Roman amphitheatre in existence, after the Colosseum and that at Capua. An earthquake in 1183 destroyed the outer arcade and only a two-storey 'wing', each of four arches, remains. This great 'wing' – and it is known as the *ala*, or wing – is very impressive, somehow dramatic, it really is like a huge stone wing soaring above the arena.

But when you have paid your admission fee at the ticket office and walk round the inner arcade it is curiously like being behind the auditorium at the Albert Hall, and, as there, steps lead up at intervals to the tiers of seats, but unlike the Albert Hall there are vast, cavernous stone arches. When you have ascended one of the flights of steps and come up into the arena the sunlight glare from the light stone of the tiers is fierce, and the bright clothes of people, scarlet and vivid yellow, green and blue, stand out vividly. On some of the lower tiers there was a good deal of litter the day I was there – cartons, broken glass, and a general mess. There is a long, shallow, sunken space in the sandy floor, in the middle of the arena, like an empty swimming pool. There are 'royal boxes' formed by the tops of massive entrance arches facing each other across the arena; they are really wide balconies above the arches. The thing to do is to climb up to the topmost tier of stone seats, and so massive are the stone benches that this is no mean feat. Once accomplished, however, the view from the topmost tier, out over the city in all directions is very fine, with the great 'wing' ruin looking across to St Peter's Castle, on its hill-top, its crenellated red roofs rising above the cypresses, and down below the Piazza Brà with its cedars and fountains and gardens, flanked by noble classical buildings. It is so beautiful a square that it should surely be made a pedestrian thoroughfare, instead of being lambasted on all sides by an un-ending, ceaseless motorcade of cars and scooters – the noise from which reaches even to the top of the Arena.

The seating accommodation in this vast amphitheatre is given variously as 22,000 and 25,000, and opera and Shakespeare are presented there in the summer, from July 15 to August 20. *Aïda* was produced there for the first time in 1913.

It is all tremendously impressive, and opera done in such a setting, particularly such a spectacular opera as *Aïda*, open to the warm Italian summer night sky, must surely seem something out of this world.

With some time in hand before joining the coach to return to Venice I went back to the Castelvecchio for another look at the Caroto painting of the young Benedictine, and the Bassetti painting of St Anthony of Padua. I wanted, also, to look at other paintings of Caroto, and did so, but nothing else of his moved me.

Above: Siena, street scene:
'narrow lanes and ancient
walls.'

*Below: Siena, inside the
cathedral*: '. . . staggering.
Black and white striped marble,
with enormous pillars.'

Siena, the Piazza del Campo: 'a shallow, fan-shaped bowl. Scene of the cele-brated horse-races, the Palio, each summer.'

Vicenza, interior of the Teatro Olimpico: 'set scenery, consisting of three moonlit streets leading up from the stage – astonishing feats of perspective.'

It was nevertheless fine to walk through the great lofty rooms again, with their abundance of treasures and their wonderful views from the deep windows, and on leaving the castle to sit once more, for a while, in the peace of the lovely garden of the forecourt.

Back at the Piazza Erbe the stalls were being dismantled and the square emptying for Saturday afternoon. Emptying of people but not of the cars and scooters hurtling nonstop along two sides of the piazza. Beautiful Verona, 'Venice without the water'; if only it could be converted into one large pedestrian thoroughfare; or the streets become canals, isolating it, as Venice is isolated, from the rest of 'car-crazy' Italy.

H

12

VENICE VIA
VICENZA

THERE were only seven passengers on the coach that came up from Milan and which I boarded in the Piazza Brà, two New Zealanders, two Americans, two Chileans, and myself; they were all couples, and middle-aged. The young hostess, when she had helped me aboard and settled me behind the Americans, told me her name was Louise Ella; later I learned that she had learned her English in Guildford. (The young hostess on the coach from Venice to Florence had learned hers in Brighton, and the young man who had assisted me in Florence had learned his in Tewkesbury, as I mentioned earlier. Why these young Italians went to these oddly assorted places to learn English I was not quite clear; something to do with where they had 'contacts' I believe.)

We left Verona at 2.40 p.m. and reached Vicenza, the 'city of Palladio', at 3.30. There is not much of interest en route – half an hour or so of somewhat featureless country, vineyards in the foreground (it is Soave country) and hills in the near distance, and then, shortly after three o'clock, there is the fortified hill-top town of Soave, lying back in the hinterland off the *autostrada*, with its dominating castle of the Scaligers, and Louise Ella, who has had nothing to do until then, rises to point it out to us. There are hills at the other side of the motorway after that, and then the modern blocks of the outskirts of Vicenza – an agricultural town, says Louise Ella, but famous also for its gold and silver work; she mentions that it came under Venetian domination, 'just like Verona'. Also, of course, that it is the city of Andrea Palladio, who, she declares, spent his life there, coming to Vicenza at the age of fifteen, and dying there in 1580, at the age of seventy-two. That he died in Vicenza in 1580 is not disputed, but where he was born is; some authorities say that he was born in Vicenza; others that he was born in Padua. Certainly he was born Andrea di Pietro, until he adopted the symbolic name of Palladio, at the insistence of his patron, the poet and connoisseur of arts, Gian Giorgio Trissino – though, again, some say that Palladio was the nickname bestowed on him by Trissino. Certainly Trissino launched him on his career by recognizing his ability when he worked as a stone mason on his – Trissino's – house in Vicenza, and taking him to Rome to study the works of the fifteenth-century architect, Bramante. Palladio died three months before finishing his last design, the Teatro Olimpico of Vicenza, and it was this, and not his masterpiece, the Basilica, which was the object of our brief halt in Vicenza.

Had I to choose between the two I would probably have settled for the theatre, for it is certainly astonishing. So much so that it is, in fact, difficult to describe it in terms that will really convey it. To say, simply, that it was 'an attempt to reconstruct a theatre in the ancient classical style' does not do so, though as a specification it is correct. It stands near the river, on the Piazza Matteotti; the interior is terrific with statuary and the foyer with marble floors, faded frescoes, pillars, and more statues. And it is all cold as a tomb, there being no heating. Inside, in the auditorium, the seats are tiers of benches, as in a Roman amphitheatre, and the ceiling is so realistic a representation of a blue sky with clouds that it is difficult to realize that it is not. At the top of the amphitheatre there are pillars, and above that a balustrade with statues. It all looks like marble, but is in fact wood, painted and decorated. The stage is a similarly elaborate structure of pillars and statuary in imitation marble, but what is really astonishing is the set scenery, consisting of three narrow streets leading up from the stage, from archways, and appearing to continue up and on into the far distance – astonishing feats of perspective, since they are, in fact, only twelve metres long. They are very ornate, with pillars and statuary, and represent the streets of Thebes; they were designed by Vincent Scamozzi for *Oedipus Rex*, the first play to be produced there. The theatre was designed for drama, Greek and Roman tragedies, but occasionally comedies are given, and then, apparently, the scenery is veiled. The acoustics are reputedly marvellous. The theatre, which accommodates 800–1000 people, is only used in the summer, since, being constructed of wood, it is considered that any form of heating would be dangerous. The street scenes convey an effect of moonlight, and shadow which is most beautiful. 'It is a Renaissance work,' said Louise Ella, adding that it is a 'combination of both'. To me it all looked extravagantly baroque, though Palladio was, to be sure, a man of the High Renaissance. It is all, anyhow, very, very astonishing.

We did not, of course, more than glimpse the wonderful Palladian city. It was not on the agenda that we should; we were on our way to Venice and had merely stopped off at Vicenza to see the theatre. But there was an impression of the remains of ancient walls, of a narrow river winding through the city, and of narrow arcaded streets. On the Piazza Matteotti (there seems to be a Piazza Matteotti everywhere in Italy, and quite right too!) there is the Museo Civico, designed by Palladio and regarded as a fine example of his work. There are statues on the façade and on the roof, and faded colouring top and bottom – all very Palladian, in fact. We had also a glimpse in passing of the so-called Basilica Palladiana, on the Piazza del Signori, a two-storey loggia built round three sides of the old Palazza Pubblico, the old town hall, and though Palladio began his career with this, in 1545, it was not finished until 1614 – that is to say, thirty-four years after his death. It is considered one of the finest works of the Renaissance.

The Palladian buildings are the great architectural treasures of Vicenza, and there are many of them. It is worth noting that an hour's walk or a 'bus from the Piazzo Duomo, takes one to Palladio's villa, the Rotonda Capra, begun by him in 1550; and many of the villas he designed for the great families of the time are to be found in the surrounding countryside, and there are organized excursions to them.

We reached Padua at 4.45, and it was my third time there; this time, however, the coach deposited us not outside the Scrovegni Chapel but in the cathedral square, at the other side of the city. A notice in the main entrance to the cathedral says that there is no admission for ladies wearing sleeveless dresses. Since, wearing a suit, I was fully sleeved I went in, and I am glad the Blue Guide describes the interior as 'ponderous', for it makes less shameful my admission that I could not at all cope with this vast church, in which even the chapels are huge and lavish; it all seemed too rich and monumental and grand – Italian catholic art at its ornate and overdone worst.

But there is at least this to be said for Padua Cathedral – it is not just a museum for tourists; Mass was being said in some of the chapels the Saturday evening I was there, and the confessionals were busy, with penitents two to a box, one at each side, and queues waiting.

I wandered away from the cathedral area and sat for a while at a café on a main street; there was plenty of traffic, but a blessed absence of scooters. There was again the feeling that I would like to know more of this city.

There was nothing of interest on the route after we left Padua. It was dusk by the time we reached Venice, and the-man-from-Sommariva was faithfully in attendance on the crowded, confusing Piazzale Roma, of which, in my by then exhausted state, I was very glad.

It was a relief to be in a motor-launch on the Grand Canal, in a city where the streets are waterways, and noisy as the Grand Canal now is, it is peaceful compared with the roaring, screaming, car-and-scooter-choked streets of Florence and Verona.

I3
SUNDAY IN
VENICE

THIS time it was not the Gritti, but the Regina Hotel, also on the Grand Canal, and when I say that in this I made a mistake it is absolutely no reflection on a fine first-class hotel, but because it was undergoing alterations and redecorations – which I knew when I declared that on my return I would like to stay there; what I did not realize was the extent to which it was out of action. I had wanted a room at the back, this time, because I had found the room on to the canal, at the Gritti, noisy, like a room on to a busy street in which the traffic continues into the small hours. The rooms at the Gritti are fully air-conditioned, so that I need not have minded keeping the windows closed at night to shut out the noise, but not being accustomed to air-conditioning, and having been brought up to the idea that not to have your bedroom window opened at night was 'stuffy', and even verging on the downright indecent, this was a Hard Thing. I had an idea, too, that it was at the Regina I had stayed in the twenties, on my first visit to Venice, so that sentiment came into my desire to stay there. The room at the back was no problem, since it was all they could offer; it was a pleasantly furnished room, and there were gladioli with the compliments of the management, but it looked into a well, from which emanated the smells of cooking. There was also the complication that although I was sleeping in the Regina I was eating in the Europa, which is also a *de luxe* hotel. The two hotels had been connected, but I never did master the intricacies of finding my way from the one to the other. But I liked the Europa; I liked its back entrance in an attractive courtyard with an ornamental well-head in the middle and walls crimsoned with virginia creeper. The entrance from the Grand Canal is rich with chandeliers and a general splendour, a quite different ambience from the gravity of the Gritti, but with its own kind of elegance, and the restaurant very pleasant, with excellent service, not as suave, perhaps, as at the Gritti, but efficient. The room service was good, too, and I was interested to note that the *petit déjeuner* was 1500 lire, which was dearer than at the Gritti. The rooms, too, cost much the same, which shows that what is 'special' about the Gritti is not just the price. I think, really, that the difference between the Gritti and other hotels of the same class is summed up in a small personal touch – that at the Gritti the wine waiter not merely opens the wine but pours the first glass and waits for your approval. There is just that difference in the matter of *perfetto servizio*.

Sunday in Venice, with nothing 'scheduled', nothing on my mind that I 'ought' to do, nothing to do but mooch – my favourite pastime. I began with the Fenice Theatre, not having seen it, and it being nearby, though, tucked away as it is, not easy to find. The Teatro La Fenice, to give it its correct name, is the oldest and largest theatre in Venice; it is late eighteenth century, but was burnt down in 1836 and rebuilt, 'with only slight alterations', says Hugh Honour. He describes the interior as 'all gilt and pink plush with cherubs swooping and soaring on the ceiling', and providing, he says, a 'perfect setting for any opera by Bellini, Donizetti or the early Verdi'. The exterior is not particularly remarkable. I noted that the cheapest seat was 800 lire and the dearest 6000. In the humble little church of San Fantin, opposite, free of tourists, people were celebrating the ten o'clock Mass.

By devious small lanes, if you keep going, you come to the wide open spaces of the Campo Manin, with a statue of Daniele Manin in the middle and an ugly modern bank building flanking one side. It is an arid place, but empty of tourists, and leads on through a squalid area of decaying houses with aspidistras and scruffy geraniums at the windows, and washing hanging out, to the Grand Canal, and the Rialto district with its famous bridge. It is a noisy, crowded, busy district but it is 'real' in the sense in which the San Marco area, milling with tourists, isn't. There are markets here, with fruit and vegetables and flowers, and cheeses and spaghetti and fish, and butchers' shops and bread shops, and splendid *alimentation*-style shops that seem to sell everything, including wine. I enjoyed strolling here; the morning was fresh and cool, and there was the lap of water against the canal quays, where the motor-launches were moored, and, because it was Sunday, there was the pleasant insistence of bells.

There were a good many people on the bridge, and a good deal of photography going on, but, as a change from the San Marco area, there were more Italian faces and voices than English, American, German. The canal was lively with the chugging of motor-launches and crowded *vaporetti*; a few gondolas, ferrying across, rocked in their wake. It is a very fine view along the canal from the Ponte di Rialto, in either direction, with palaces on either hand. There are shops on the bridge, as on Florence's Ponte Vecchio – which if Palladio's design had been accepted there wouldn't have been. The design accepted was by a much less distinguished architect, Antonio da Ponte, and Hugh Honour says that it is hard to see why his was preferred, 'save that it combined the function and outline of the old bridge with a modicum of classical decoration'. There were a series of wooden bridges before the present structure, which was built at the end of the sixteenth century. It is not beautiful, I suppose; the Blue Guide observes, austerely, that it is 'notable rather for strength than for grace', but I like the curved sweep of it, and the arches, and the steps, and I find I am supported in this by Ruskin, who wrote in his classic, *The Stones of Venice*, that it is 'very noble in its simplicity, in its proportions, and in its masonry'. He insisted that both the Rialto Bridge and the Bridge of Sighs are *more* than bridges (the italicization is his) 'the one a covered passage, the other a row of shops sustained on an arch'. Ruskin invites the traveller to 'note also the sculpture of the Annunciation on the southern side', but this, I am afraid, I did not note, being more interested in the

Sunday crowd, the movement on the water, and the wonderful views along the canal.

'What news on the Rialto?' Shylock, changing the subject, demanded of Bassanio, but he meant the district, not the bridge; which somehow seems a pity; it is more interesting to iamgine Venetians gathered for gossip on the bridge. Whether Shakespeare was ever himself in Venice, or anywhere in Italy, is debatable.

I, anyhow, was very happy to be 'on the Rialto', in the market place, the narrow streets, and on the bridge, that October Sunday morning.

I did not, on that occasion, go beyond the Ponte Rialto – 'that bridge of all bridges', as J. E. Morpurgo calls it in his preface to that lovely picture book of Venice he did with Martin Hürlimann – but when I had had my fill of it made my way back, deviously, to San Marco. By then the bright day had clouded over and the sky was ominous with rain coluds.

In the Piazza camera-slung tourists milled and milled around, and because it was midday there was an immense concatenation of bells. Crowds gathered below the great clock tower – late fifteenth century – to watch and wait for the two giant bronze figures, the '*mori*', the Moors, to strike the hour on the great bell. Above the clock face on the tower is a gilded Madonna, and above that the winged lion of Venice against a blue background studded with golden stars. Visitors may ascend the tower, and back in the twenties I did, and was tremendously impressed by the ruggedness of the mighty, half-naked Moors, most powerfully equipped . . . about which we, who were young then, were most excruciatingly broad-minded.

This time I did not ascend but sat on a stone bench facing across to the tower and watched the crowds and looked at the wonderful bronze horses above the central porch of the Basilica, the famous *quadriga*, spoils from Constantinople in the thirteenth century, and still with traces of the original gilding, most marvellously lit up when the sunlight touches them. There was a great babble of voices, but it was still mainly Italian. It was Sunday morning in Venice, with the world and his wife strolling in the square, with the tourists as incidental as the pigeons, and many fewer than in September.

If you walk down the Piazzetta, the smaller square leading off from the Piazza, the main square, to the waterfront, the Molo, a principal gondola and motor-launch station, and turn left past the Doges' Palace, continuing along the Molo, you come to a graceful, stone-balustraded bridge, with steps up and down, over a small canal; this is the Ponte della Paglio, and the canal is the Rio di Palazzo, and the bridge over it, a roofed-over, clumsy structure with barred windows, is the famous Bridge of Sighs, the Ponte dei Sospiri, a covered way used to transfer prisoners from the Prigioni, the State prison, at one side of the canal, to the Doges' Palace, at the other – Byron's 'a palace and a prison on each hand' – to be examined by the State Inquisitors.

James Morris refers to Byron's 'sentimental but misinformed reverie' on the Bridge of Sighs, and Hugh Honour says that in fact only one political prisoner ever passed across the bridge, and that for this reason the American writer, W. D. Howells, who was United States consul in Venice before he became a novelist, called it a 'pathetic swindle'. For my part I am only too glad to be assured that it is. I often looked at the heavily barred windows of the prison, the lowest only a few feet above the canal, and wondered about the dungeons behind. Dickens inspected them and wrote of them with horror, but according to Hugh Honour, Casanova, who made a daring escape from the prison, records that he passed a 'relatively happy confinement' therein, 'diverting himself with the records of a scabrous lawsuit among the archives in an adjoining room'. The Blue Guide says that the two lowest storeys were reserved for the most dangerous criminals, adding that the lowest of them was not below street level, and that 'they were less terrible than the usual medieval prison'; Hugh Honour that they were 'no less hygienic than those in nineteenth-century England', which, to my anti-prison mind, is not saying much.

For Dickens, whose social conscience was acute, though Venice was an architectural dream of beauty the prisons were a nightmare.

Beyond the Ponte della Paglia stretches the long promenade of the Riva degli Schiavoni, where the crowds thin out. They thin out because the touristic excitement ends at the Ponte della Paglia and the Bridge of Sighs. Once you have descended to the other side of the Ponte della Paglia you have left behind the whole San Marco area – the Piazza, the Piazzetta, the Doge's Palace, the Molo – and are thus out of the Tourist Belt.

There is nothing spectacular or of touristic or cultural interest along the broad Schiavoni, but it is a pleasant walk if you like waterfronts and shipping. You cross a canal or two, go up and down a bridge or two, and come eventually to the Arsenale and the Naval Museum and the Riva S. Biagio, where, on that Sunday morning, there was at the quayside an American battleship called the *Graham County*, which seemed all Stars-and-Stripes and clusters of lost-looking American sailors. There were also ships of the Italian Navy, a Greek tourist ship, and various other ships whose nationalities and business I could not make out. But everywhere *ships* – and I am of those who find waterfronts with ships of all nations exciting.

It is a scruffy area of shabby houses and side-streets with washing hanging out, strung from side to side, from each floor; there are no palaces here, but a church or two. It is one of the non-touristic aspects of Venice.

After the Naval Museum you cross another bridge over another canal and are on the Riva del 7 Martiri, though who were the seven martyrs I do not know and cannot discover. Anyhow, at the end of that waterfront you cross the Viale Garibaldi and come to the public gardens, the Giardini Pubblici, which were really the objective of that Sunday-morning stroll out along the Riva Schiavoni and beyond.

I had, somehow, not really believed that there were public gardens – anyhow as we in England understood the term – in Venice. There are some small gardens round the corner from San Marco, I know, with trees and grass and flower beds of a kind, but something very much less than what in England we should call 'public gardens'. I had been assured that there were real public gardens in Venice, and that they were to be found out there beyond the Museo Navale. It is true, too. There are public gardens, laid out in 1807, by Napoleon. I did not, however, think much of these Giardini Pubblici. To me they seemed nothing very much, a bit 'French', and arid. There was a darkness of ilex trees, a few small palms, statuary surrounded by beds of begonias, benches on which men sat reading newspapers. There were swings, seesaws, and a slide for children. In the summer they provide a cool shade, of course precious in so treeless a place; that October morning they seemed to have nothing much to offer. There were, of course cats. Wherever there are a few trees and shrubs and a patch of grass in Venice there are cats.

Something has to be said about the cats of Venice, but I must say at the outset that I am not amongst those who find them an attractive aspect of Venetian life. I do not find them fascinating, but only pitiable, and their homeless existence deplorable. That many of them are fine-looking creatures I would not deny, nor that in general they look 'all right'; they do not, that is to say, appear to be starving. But a cat is either wild, as I have seen them in the Indian jungles, or it is domesticated; the cats of Venice are not wild cats, but, simply, homeless domestic cats. In some fashion they get by, foraging in dustbins, and fed by cat-loving tourists. Cats, with their nine lives, have that capacity for somehow surviving. But they deserve better. Heavens, how *much* creatures so beautiful, so proudly independent, so courageous, deserve better!

James Morris writes at some length in his book, *Venice*, about the cats, and he would undoubtedly regard my own attitude as grossly sentimental, since he does not find them at all in need of pity. 'For myself,' he writes, 'I love the cats of Venice, peering from their pedestals, sunning themselves on the feet of statues, crouching on dark staircases to escape the rain, or gingerly emerging into the daylight from their fetid subterranean lairs.' Most, he says are only half-domesticated, living on charity, and 'you may see them any morning wolfing the entrails, fish-tails and *pasta*, wrapped in newspapers, which householders have laid down for them'. You see them all right, everywhere, striped and plain, ginger and tortoise-shell, movingly beautiful as cats always are, and, I will admit, in general not in bad shape, but I could never feel other than worried about them – being of those who will always worry about a cat.

I worried about the hordes of obviously starving cats at the pigeon restaurants along the Nile in Cairo (restaurants which serve only pigeon), thin, desperate creatures fighting savagely over the bones flung to them by diners. I worried over the cats prowling in the public gardens in the South of France. I worried about cats amongst the ruins of castles in hot Jordanian deserts. I have worried about cats all over the world, it seems to me, and despite the fact that they didn't look in too bad shape I worried about the cats in Venice.

I had heard about elderly English women who went about Venice feeding the cats, but in all my wanderings I only saw two women feeding cats, middle-aged rather than elderly, but of what nationality I do not know. I saw a woman pushing food through a grille in a window that opened on to a narrow lane, and a kitten eating on the sill inside. I saw a woman put down a paper of food in another lane – and the cat she was coaxing came and looked at it and sniffed it and walked away.

Some years ago I read about Englishwomen who were combining into some sort of committee or society to rescue the cats of Venice – to the intense annoyance of the Municipal Authorities who told them, in effect, to mind their own business and go away. No more was heard of the venture, and despite my empathy with cats I find myself on the side of the Venetian Authorities; it is probably very much better to be an alley cat in Venice than be rescued by some English do-gooder lady . . . and what? Taken to some animal welfare centre and finally be what is euphemistically called 'put down'?

According to Mary McCarthy the Venetians are fond of pets and prefer cats to dogs, 'which are impractical in a city which has so little open space'. But there are all the wide-open spaces of all those *campos*, not to mention all those broad waterfronts; but where is there in Venice for a decent cat to scratch a hole? Only the little nothing of a garden round the corner from San Marco, and the shrubberies of the Giardini Pubblici – way out beyond the Schiavoni. Oh yes, to be sure, there are the little hidden patios behind high walls, strictly private, and the terrain of the fat, well-fed resident cat.

James Morris, who lived there, declares that there are hundreds of gardens hidden among the stones of Venice, but admits that they are mostly 'jealously locked, and impenetrable to strangers'; he speaks of them as 'haunted by cats', but they would be inaccessible to the cats who haunt the quays and hang about, hopefully, round the cafés and lurk in the dingy shrubberies of the public gardens.

Back on the Schiavoni I had the good fortune to arrive at the Ponte della Pietà just in time to see a wedding-party gondola approaching across the lagoon and glide under the bridge. There were two gondoliers, white-clad and wearing broad red sashes, and with red ribbons streaming from the backs of their wide-brimmed straw hats. The gondola was furnished with special ornamental chairs for the bridal couple, and baskets of white gladioli were stacked up behind them. The bridegroom was a handsome young man and the bride a very pretty girl, and both smiled up happily at the laughing, waving, camera-clicking crowd on the bridge. Excited, yelling children climbed up on to the balustrade, and the crowd, surging from one side of the bridge to the other as the gondola glided under, was full of that excited pleasure that weddings everywhere invoke. The gondoliers brought the boat to a flight of steps in front of a house, where some people waited, and the lovely little bride was handed out. She stepped out gracefully, the train of her white dress and the ends of her flowing veil trailing on the pavement. A motor-launch with white ribbons and white flowers on the roof of the cabin chugged up with a party of wedding guests. An Italian family, parents and children, picnicked on some steps just below the bridge, complete with a bottle of wine, and what might be called a grandstand view of the proceedings.

A little farther on, at the Ponte del Vin, I arrived just in time for another wedding party! This time the white-clad gondoliers wore broad gold sashes, with hat ribbons to match, and the bride, though all in white, had no veil, but her hair was bedecked with white flowers, and she, too, was very pretty, and her groom good-looking – but the standard of looks in young Italians is in general, high. This bride also held up her train as she stepped from the gondola on to steps in front of a house to be received by waiting guests. This was not such a 'pretty wedding', but it was a pleasant sight all the same.

Incredibly at the next bridge, the Ponte della Paglia, there was a third wedding party, but this time much less romantic, as the bridal couple arrived by motor-launch, and it all passed too quickly under the bridge to excite much attention.

But whilst I was watching I heard my name called, 'Miss Mannin! Miss Mannin!' and that seemed as incredible as three weddings in one morning. Turning, confusedly, I found myself accosted by the pleasant, middle-aged New Zealanders who had been on the coach from Verona.

'You remember us?' the woman cried, eagerly.

I did, of course. We had chatted a little, on the coach, and at Vicenza. They were going on next day to Florence – after two nights and a day in Venice. Such is tourism. But central to my philosophy is the belief that something is always better than nothing. They would at least have seen the Byzantine dream of beauty that is San Marco, and for that alone they could intone, 'Blessed are mine eyes . . .'

The man was less excited. He had been in Venice before. As though once was enough. Or would anyhow do very well. They were going out to the lagoon islands in the afternoon, the woman said. Should be nice, I responded, not having been myself. Well, nice to have seen you again. Look out for the book. We will, of course. Good-bye, good-bye. No *arrivederci* about it. How could there be? I didn't even know their name.

Then, as though three wedding parties and an encounter were not enough, opposite the Doges' Palace a regatta of gondolas was being launched. They were very superior gondolas, large and very ornate, and manned by four or more gondoliers in different coloured costumes – red, violet, blue, yellow – and it was all very spectacular, and in front of the ducal palace were tiers of seats, with a bank of flowers below. It looked all very interesting; but it also looked as though the heavens would open at any moment and wash it all out. The rain did in fact set in mid-afternoon, with so great a thunderstorm that I wondered whether the Piazza San Marco would be flooded again; but the regatta, I imagined, would have been over by then.

I inquired at the hotel about the event, and was told that it was held annually, in aid of charity – a home or school for handicapped children, or something of the kind. The gondoliers raced from San Marco to the Ponte Rialto, and they wore the different coloured costumes for obvious distinguishing reasons, as jockeys do in horse-races.

I pondered, afterwards, in what way this gondola race benefited charity, since anyone could view it at any point along the Grand Canal; I could only conclude that at the start and finish there were tiers of seats, such as those at the side of the Doges' Palace, for which a charge was made, and that there were a sufficient number of people who liked to sit and watch it all in comfort, instead of just standing about on the Molo or at the Rialto. It certainly presented a fine spectacle, that great concourse of gondolas.

I was glad to have had a glimpse of the regatta, and the thunderstorm made a dramatic finale to what might be called a 'rich and full' Sunday morning in Venice.

Verona, the Arena: 'at the city's heart, and its most important monument. Wonderful view from the top.'

The Ponte di Castelvecchio: 'fantastic because so massive, so crenellated, so lavish with towers, so exaggeratedly medieval.'

Above: Murano: 'Looking along the Grand Canal to the Ponte Vivarini. I liked it in Murano, even though every other shop is a glass shop.'

Left: Torcello, the cathedral and the church of St Fosca: 'People cross the lagoon for the mosaics in the cathedral and the good food at the sophisticated restaurant nearby . . .'

14

CA' D'ORO, 'HOUSE
OF GOLD'

WHEN a guide book one respects as much as I respect the Blue
Guide insists that the Ca' d'Oro is the 'most beautiful Gothic
building in Venice', you know, if you are being 'conscientious'
about Venice, that it is something you must see. I therefore
peered at the map and, inveterate foot-slogger that I am, plotted a
course for it; needlessly – since there is a *vaporetto* that goes to it
from the San Marco stop.

It entailed, I perceived, trekking back to the Rialto, and it was,
apparently, some way beyond the bridge, and it proved to be a not
very interesting walk, though, as I recorded in my notes, 'tourist
free'. It is not easy to find this 'House of Gold' on the Grand Canal;
it is down a narrow alleyway, the Calle della Ca' d'Oro, off the broad
Strada Nuova – where, confusingly, there is a shop calling itself
Ca' d'Oro. A small yellow notice high on the wall in the alleyway
is easy to miss and might as well not be there as a guide to the Casa.

Anyhow, I finally found it, and the entrance to it is in the narrow
lane, the Calle della Ca' d'Oro. The entrance . . . but inscribed on
a wooden door set in a stone entrance arch were the words: *Fermée,
Geschlossen, Lerrada, Closed*. For '*restauration*'.

Above this closed-in-four-languages doorway was a notice
which declared in plain English that the Galleria Giorgio Franchetti,
contained within the Ca' d'Oro, was 'exclusively financed by the
Ministero Pubblica Istruzione-Direzione Belle Arti'. Which I
take to mean financed by the Ministry of Fine Arts.

I walked to the end of the narrow lane, to the canal, and peered
round to see the façade of this so relentlessly closed building. It is

I

not, however, a good angle from which to view it, and I only really saw it when I got the *vaporetto* from there back to St Mark's. From the water it is seen to be very beautiful indeed, though the gilding which gave the house its name in the fifteenth century vanished long ago. The first and second floors are loggias, the pillars supporting ornate and delicate stonework, and there are balconied Gothic windows. The house has had many changes of ownership since it was built for the Contarini family between 1420 and 1434, but was finally rescued and restored by Baron Franchetti in 1922 and presented to the nation, along with his collection of paintings and antiquities which now constitute the Galleria Franchetti. The most famous of the paintings is Mantegna's Sebastian, left unfinished at his death in 1506. James Morris records that it was found in his studio after his death, and 'that at the foot of the picture, beside a smoking candle-wick', is the inscription, *'Nil Nisi Divinum Stabile Est, Caetera Fumus* – Nothing But God Endures, The Rest Is Smoke'. I think I might not have liked the Sebastian – all those arrows! – but I would have liked the ancient well-head in the entrance courtyard, and the portico with the antique sculpture, and the view of the Grand Canal from the loggia on the first floor. There are many fine buildings along the canal, at both sides, just there, a succession of palaces, and blue and white painted mooring posts bring colour to the scene. It is, in my opinion, one of the most attractive parts of the Grand Canal, though my favourite view will always be over the red and white posts at Accademia bridge looking down to the domes of the Santa Maria della Salute.

There is no better way, really, to see the Grand Canal than by *vaporetto*, for it zigzags from side to side, stopping at all the stops, pleasantly leisurely.

On the journey from the Ca' d'Oro to San Marco you cover the main part of the Grand Canal, passing under the Ponte Rialto and sweeping round in an S-bend to the Ponte Accademia, with palaces on either hand, all the way. It is only be traversing this stretch that it is possible to realize the full magnificence of this unique waterway. It is not necessary to be able to identify all the palaces – who lived in them, for whom they were built, and when, or be knowledgeable about their architectural styles; if you can it adds to their interest, but it cannot add anything to their beauty; for the unknowledgeable, such as myself, it is sufficient that they stand there with their feet in the water and that their façades are beautiful with delicate stone-work traceries, and romantic with loggias with decorated pillars.

But for those who like the particulars – at the Palazzo Mocenigo, before you reach the Accademia Bridge, coming from the Rialto, Byron wrote the beginning of *Don Juan* in 1818 and entertained Thomas Moore. Farther up the canal, beyond the Rialto and the Ca' d'Oro, is the Palazzo Vendramin-Calargi where Wagner died, as a commemorative plaque on the garden wall, written by d'Annunzio, records; the building is considered the finest Lombardesque palace in Venice. Wagner wrote the second act of *Tristan* at another palace, the fifteenth-century Gothic Guistiniani, lower down the Canal, on the other bank, near the Accademia Bridge and the Palazzo Rezzonico in which Robert Browning stayed for a while – his son having bought the place – and died. At the Europa Hotel, just beyond San Marco, for which I was heading in the crowded *vaporetto*, on the way back from the Ca' d'Oro, Verdi stayed in 1851 for the rehearsals of *Rigoletto* at the Fenice.

The Grand Canal is the 'High Street' of Venice. It is two-and-a-half miles long, and, as has been pointed out, offers the only long, uninterrupted view. It is wide and busy, and in recent years noisy with motor traffic, but remains a most beautiful thoroughfare whether sparkling in sunshine or wildly Gothic in the rain.

15

THE ISLANDS OF THE LAGOON

In the afternoon of that day when I arrived at the Ca' d'Oro only to find it closed I made the mistake of going on an *excursione* to the islands of the lagoon. It was a mistake for two reasons: firstly that on this excursion the visit to Murano is null and void, since the excursionists are taken only to a glass factory and see nothing at all of the island; secondly that it costs fifteen hundred lire, whereas by *vaporetto* the fare is only one hundred and twenty, and by using public transport you are free to spend as much or little time at each island, Murano, Burano, and Torcello, as you please, since there is a regular *vaporetto* service to and from.

Anyhow, I made that mistake and went by *motoscafo*, and though it meant I had to go again, *properly*, by *vaporetto*, there was a sense in which it was not completely a dead loss, for though I set out by *motoscafo* I did not, as it turned out, return by it, and the occasion was therefore by way of being a small adventure.

A *motoscafo* is a largish motor-launch; the 'taxi' motor-launch is something different, with only a small cabin capable of accommodating at most four persons, and being 'private' is expensive; where – as the *motoscafo* is public, like a small-scale *vaporetto*. But that afternoon, wandering along the Molo, I saw this excursion advertised on a placard, visiting all the islands, leaving at 2.30 p.m., and it being then 2.25 p.m. I thought, why not? and paid my fifteen hundred lire at the receipt of custom. I should have known better.

The launch was full, despite the fact that it was a wet afternoon. There was a marked absence of English or Americans on board, and at first I thought the company was entirely Italian except for myself, but later a German presence was revealed.

The first call was at a glass-factory quayside at Murano. There was a brief visit to the furnace – little more than a walk-through – and a very much more lesiurely walk-through the show-rooms . . . which did not seem productive of sales. Some of the Murano glass is beautiful – and expensive; a good deal of it is excessively vulgar, and though it is cheap is not worth buying. Many people, bored, like myself, returned to the launch early, having seen nothing at all of the island of Murano, the largest of the islands of the north of the lagoon.

At three-forty-five we reached Burano, on which we had half an hour. Perhaps half an hour is enough for Burano, since there is really nothing to it but a broad, cobbled main street with red-roofed and variously painted houses – mauve, red, pink; there is a canal, and out in the lagoon there are fishing-boats, and fish-traps like lobster baskets, and there is a big square full of playing children, and a church, and the church and square are ugly, but there is a feeling of life. There are lace shops and lace stalls – Burano is as famous for its lace as Murano for its glass – and there is an ugly, strictly utilitarian, fountain in the ugly square. The most attractive view of Burano is from the lagoon, from which, with its variously coloured houses and its fishing boats it has a certain charm; in my opinion the charm diminishes on closer inspection, though Burano, it is only fair to add, is generally regarded as 'picturesque'.

We were delayed in leaving Burano by three Germans, a middle-aged woman and two men, who had had a row with an Italian couple when we left Murano, accusing them of taking their seats, and who were now engaged in a row with a lace-seller.

The row was conducted in German; the Frau, who was doing most of the talking, clutched some lace mats in one hand and waved the other, angrily, at a young Italian woman and two Italian young men; the Frau railed and railed; the Italians smiled, and smiled. Finally, at the insistence of the driver of the *motoscafo* the Germans came aboard, and the Italians walked away, laughing . . . Whatever the altercation was about – and I suppose it was about the price of the lace mats – it would appear that they had won. I found myself wondering what pleasure those lace mats, bought at Burano, would give that Frau X, when she returned home, always reminding her of the row. I wondered about the life on Burano. James Morris writes romantically about the island, as a 'sheer splash of colour', with the women leaning over the lace-making frame and the men paddling out to the mudbanks to fish, but he does add that the drainage is the 'filthiest and smelliest in the lagoon', and that the streets are 'thick with muck'. I saw only the broad main street, with its small shops full of postcards, Murano glass – much of it ugly and vulgar – and lace. At 4 p.m. there was a concatenation of bells from two churches, and a scurry of children scampering in the square, rounded up by a black-robed priest.

At four-twenty-five, ten minutes late, due to the altercation between the Germans and the lace-maker, we took off for the 'loneliest island' of the lagoon, Torcello. There were islets of coarse grass everywhere, and a tall square campanile in the near-distance, and I recorded in my notes that it was 'all strange and marshy and lost, and desolate under the dark sky'.

We stepped ashore from the *motoscafo* at a small landing-stage and followed the guide, a multilingual young woman, along a narrow footpath through a thin wood of acacia trees and elders and thorn bushes, in the shadow of the campanile, to the cathedral – the famous largely ninth-century basilica of Santa Maria Assunta . . . to which there is an admission fee of 100 lire, which I, anyhow, resented, since the place is not entirely a museum but still used occasionally as a church.

The interior is remarkable, being entirely of brick, even around the huge altar; there are even brick steps up behind the bishop's wooden throne. It is gaunt and barn-like, and would be hideous but for the mosaics, which are startling, and sometimes strangely beautiful. I made a few notes: *Altar*, seventh century; original. To the right of the altar a remarkable ninth-century mosaic of Christ with archangels and saints. *Roof*, arched; twelfth-century mosaics. *Crypt*, down a flight of steps; flooded. Tremendous mosaic of the *Last Judgement* on the wast wall; Byzantine, twelfth–thirteenth century. Impressive.'

(According to the Official Guide, 'The mosaics of Torcello represent the continuation of the Ravenna school of mosaic decoration transferred to the lagoons, and prepare the way for the iconography and technique of the mosaics of St Mark's.')

The young guide from the *motoscafo* rattled it all off in English, German, French, Italian. We gathered round her, serious and intent, but I cannot say that I registered very much. The 'official guide' method is a singularly ineffective means of communication, in my opinion and experience. But it needed no guide to point out the lovely Madonna and Child at the other end of the church, a tall, and movingly human, blue-clad figure against a shining golden background.

There are other fine mosaics, but these are the most remarkable and memorable.

We were conducted outside, to the south side of the cathedral, to be shown the shutters of the windows – remarkable because formed of hinged stone slabs.

We emerged into a small piazza, enclosed by ancient buildings, and at one side a restaurant. At the side of a grassy verge leading away from the piazza women stood behind stalls – lace stalls, postcard and souvenir stalls. In the middle of the square there is a kind of stone seat, known as Attila's Chair, and there is a small museum, with steps up to the first floor, and a bell tower – it was once the palace of Government. All this I glimpsed, and I wanted to know more about it all, but the party was already on the way back to the *motoscafo*; I ran back to the cathedral to buy a booklet I had noticed on sale in the porch. Then I ran back to rejoin the party.

I had to run to catch up with them, and my running led me along a narrow canal, and I did not remember that we traversed a canal when we left the launch, and I did not recognize any of the party.

I had, in fact, in my anxiety to catch up, tacked on to the wrong party.

I panted along the canal and finally caught up with some women. I said, 'I don't remember that we came along a canal – '

One of the women said, amiably, with a marked North Country accent, 'You couldn't have noticed, love.'

'I came on a launch called the *Marco Polo*,' I said. 'Was that the launch you came on?'

'I don't know, love. We were with a party. Were you with a party?'

So that was it, then. I was lost. I was now with a party. But by whatever vessel they were returning on they had to have me – even if I had to cling on to the side. In retrospect I don't know why I panicked so, except that that tiny, marshy, reedy island seemed most desperately forlorn and lost – *dreary*; no place to be marooned on. (I did not know, then, but the restaurant I had noticed on the Piazza is also a good hotel – the Locanda Cipriani, run by Cipriani of Harry's Bar in Venice, and tourists come out from Venice, on launches from Harry's Bar, just to lunch there, and they have a quick run-round the cathedral, and return to Venice thinking Torcello *marvellous* . . .)

As I trekked along with the ladies from the North I heard the *motoscafo* blasting on its siren, far away, calling to the missing passenger that was me that departure was imminent. *Mournful*, and for one wild moment I had the idea of turning and pelting back along the canal to the cathedral and the little landing-stage, but realized that if I did I would almost certainly arrive too late for the *Marco Polo*, and then get back too late for the vessel – whatever it was – the party I had tacked on to was making for.

What we were making for, at the point at which the canal flowed out into the lagoon, was a *vaporetto* stop. It seemed to me odd that the ladies wouldn't know they had come out by *vaporetto*, but evidently they only knew that they had boarded a boat of some kind, having been shepherded aboard, and now were returning on a boat of some kind, as per instructions. A man in the party observed to me that he understood that the boat we were returning on didn't go to San Marco – that we had to change. I was not much interested.

The thing was to get back to Venice, and one *vaporetto* stop would serve as well as another, I thought, recklessly.

The *vaporetto* was crowded – well, they always are. I got a Campari at a bar, and found a seat in a smoky lounge in which there was a good deal of noisy card-playing by Italian young men. A middle-aged Italian, a business type, was necking madly with a girl young enough to be his daughter, though they sat at a table with people sitting across from them. I wearied of the embarrassing spectacle, and of the smoke, and the noise, and went out on deck. The lagoon was marked out by posts into routes, and signposted, as though it were terra firma. We called at Murano Faro, with its black and white striped lighthouse, and passed close to the cemetery island of San Michele, enclosed by red brick walls and thick with tall cypresses.

When we came to Venice, and it was all change, I was convinced that the stop was at the Public Gardens, and was resolved not to bother with another *vaporetto* – I could easily walk. I had been going for some minutes before I realized that I was not on the Riva of the Seven Martyrs; that I was not anywhere I knew, and where I was I had no idea at all, and it was by then dark. I accosted a man and he understood that I inquired for the direction of San Marco. He threw up his arms in astonishment and though I did not understand his words I very clearly understood that I was certainly not heading in that direction. He went on talking and gesticulating, and I understood that I should accompany him, and we went up steps and down steps, over little bridges, over little canals, and Santa Maria Formosa, he repeated, Campo Santa Maria Formosa. Finally he stopped and waved me on. I thanked him and went on in the direction he had indicated, along narrow lanes, and up steps and down steps, and nothing was recognizable and there was no Campo Santa Maria Formosa, and I was utterly and completely lost. There were also no people in all those alleyways to inquire of – until, at last, a portly elderly Franciscan came flapping along in his brown robes. '*Scusi*,' 'I said again, and '*direzione* San Marco,' and for full measure threw in the Campo Santa Maria Formosa. His reaction was reassuringly positive, his manner kindly, and he indicated that I should accompany him . . . and we went up steps and down steps, over little bridges, over little canals, and he went on talking, soothingly, explanatorily – if only I could have understood. At a crossroads of narrow streets he halted and waved me on, straight ahead, very clearly. 'Santa Maria Formosa,' he said, and something about San Marco. I thanked him, warmly, and was troubled that he then turned and went back in the direction by which we had come, realizing that he had gone out of his way to set me on mine . . . as the Sermon on the Mount commands, for the practising Christian.

I continued on, and I came at last to the Campo Santa Maria Formosa, and at a kiosk at the perimeter inquired of some young men for San Marco, and gathered that it was close at hand, and by way of the busy shopping street of the Merceria came out into the Piazza. It was by then seven o'clock and I was very tired. It was two hours since I had left Torcello.

Back in my room at the hotel I studied the map. It seemed the *vaporetto*, Linea 12, had arrived at the Fondamenta Nuove, at the north side of the city. Had I changed there with the party we would have taken the short cut through to the Grand Canal and followed the S-curve round to San Marco.

Well, it had been interesting, but I could hardly have been said to have seen the islands. I wanted to see Murano, and there must surely be more to Torcello. I resolved to go again – by *vaporetto*.

I made my way back next day to the Fondamenta Nuove via the Rialto, to avoid the Merceria, which is low and narrow and congested, a kind of crowded high street, with fruit and vegetable shops, butchers, pâtisseries, snack-bars, dress shops, and the everlasting glass shops all selling the same things, until you are sick of the sight of them. The Rialto route takes you via San Canciano, the church and the square, and you come eventually to the Calle Larga Botteri, from which three narrow lanes lead to the *fondamenta*, and the second to the Murano *vaporetto* stop.

In exactly one hour from leaving the hotel I stepped ashore at Murano, but it is only a very short trip, after calling first at San Michele. Hugh Honour wrote of a visit to Murano that the 'whole island seems alive with touts enticing visitors into the [glass] factories'. This was not my experience, but it depends, I imagine, on the time of the year; I was there in October and walked unmolested along the pleasant broad pavement of the Vetrai Canal, where almost every shop is, as might be expected, a glass shop. No need, however, to look at the shop windows; there is a busyness of boats and barges along the canal, and there are small café-bars, and the sombre-looking church of St Peter the Martyr. Across St Peter's Bridge there is the Campo San Stefano, with a nineteenth-century campanile.

More interesting is the Ponte Vivarini across the Grand Canal; it is an ugly iron bridge, but it has the handsome Palazzo da Mula at one side, 'one of the few traces of Murano's ancient splendour', says the Blue Guide. The prows of some of the boats moored here, along the Fondamenta Venier, are elaborately painted with designs of flowers and angels blowing trumpets. The houses are multi-coloured, as of Burano, and crimson virginia creeper falls in long loose trails over walls. There is a convent school, a square white building with an avenue of acacia trees leading up to it, and at one side a playground where white-overalled children play on swings and seesaws and small roundabouts, supervised by white-robed nuns. There are the cries of the playing children, and the chug of barges and launches on the canal. At the end of the *fondamenta* there are villas, half hidden among flowering oleanders and clumps of sunflowers and vines. Across the water from them are furnaces, and there are furnaces near by. Well, but it *is* Murano.

Continuing on along the *fondamenta* you come to the big church which is visible from the Ponte Vivarini, an impressive sight with its long red roof and its campanile. I had regarded it with interest from the bridge and been anxious to reach it believing it to be the basilica, but it is not, but the church of Santa Maria degli Angeli I learned from a friendly woman of whom I inquired. She told me something about it, something which, from the manner of its telling, seemed explanatory, but which was lost to me, not understanding Italian. What she was explaining to me was that the church is no longer in use – which is immediately evident as soon as you pass into the grassy, litter-strewn precincts beyond an entrance arch above which there is an almost effaced bas-relief of the Annunciation. There is what would seem to be an ancient stone font in the middle of the waste ground. There was not a pane of glass left in any of the windows, the plaster was peeling from the campanile, and there was a general air of desuetude. How long it has been in this condition I do not know, but Hugh Honour, writing in 1965, has nothing to say about it except that the convent beside it was the scene of one of Casanova's more colourful adventures.*

It is hot and shadeless at this side of the canal and I walk back to the Ponte Vivarini, where a barge laid out as a fish shop is moored, and women are gathered on the quay with their shopping bags and baskets. At the other side of the bridge, where the *fondamenta* is in the shade, there is a mosaic Madonna on the wall of a house; it is railed off, and a little lamp burns in front of the mosaic, and small vases of roses are set at either side. The date on this attractive little shrine is 1954. Beyond the house there is the entrance yard to a glass factory.

Whilst I stand inspecting the Madonna there is a blast of sirens, announcing noon, and a clamour of church bells, and a sudden streaming-out of people from the glass factories, both men and women, but mostly men, wearing a kind of working uniform of blue cotton shirts, and all of them hurrying across the bridge, in

---

* On my return to London I took the matter up with the Italian State Tourist Office, who in turn took it up with the Venetian authorities, who looked into it, agreed that it is windowless and neglected, and have 'asked for the intervention of the competent authorities so that something might be done about this state of affairs, which,' they add, with good Italian realism, 'certainly does not help Venice tourism' (*'che non depone certamente a favore del turismo veneziano'*).

both directions, going home to lunch. An hour later there is the return flow.

I liked it in Murano, though I did not do either of the things it is proper to do there – that is to say visit the glass museum, the Museo dell'Arte Vetraria, nor the basilica of Santi Maria e Donato, the one because I was not much inclined, the other because Italian churches close at midday and do not reopen until around four, which meant that I was there at the wrong time. The church is twelfth century, and it is close to the museum; it has been clumsily restored, and the exterior is ugly, but inside there are twelfth-century mosaics, and a remarkable floor. The museum contains glass from early Egyptian to the present day, and is reputedly one of the largest Venetian glass collections in the world. The building which houses it is the Palazzo Giustiniani, built for the bishops of Torcello towards the end of the seventeenth century. It is worth noting that the museum closes at 12.30 and reopens at 2.30.

The museum, of course, contains fine examples of sixteenth-century Venetian glass, wonderful goblets, chandeliers, mirrors, and very beautiful Venetian glass is still produced today, so that it is just a pity that most of what clutters the shops in Venice and Murano for the tourist trade, is so incredibly vulgar – all those spindly-legged horses and deer, all those pop-eyed clowns and coons and harlequins and grotesque cats, in horrible crude colours, all those pointless swans, all those gilded goblets – travesties of an exquisite and ancient art.

By twelve-thirty I was back in Venice, at the Fondamenta Nuove, then, because a *vaporetto* was about to leave for Torcello, I boarded it – there had to be more to Torcello than a Byzantine cathedral, an expensive, sophisticated restaurant, and a narrow canal, and I had to know.

I have to report that there *is* a little more than that, but not much. There is the curiously shaped brick-built church of Santa Fosca, beside the cathedral, early eleventh century and octagonal, stark inside with brick and columns; there are the waterlogged ruins – really only the foundations – of the convent to St John the Evangelist; and the hump-backed Devil's Bridge across the canal, which I did notice on my first visit, but was too agitated, as I scampered along, to see as more than a small brick bridge, without balustrades, leading to what seemed to be a scruffy looking area of undefined cultivation, with a small vineyard in the foreground.

This time, alighting from the *vaporetto* and taking my time along the footpath beside the canal, I not only observed it but crossed it. It leads to allotment-like fields of artichokes, all very rough and dreary, and seeming to lead nowhere. The bridge itself is small and low and arched, with broad brick steps leading up and down. From it there is a good view of the cathedral and the campanile in the near distance. Beside it there is a small café-bar, at which I briefly sat, at a table outside, drinking Campari and feeding most of some tough *pizza* to a gaunt one-eyed female cat and a thin kitten. At that side of the canal there is a wasteland of marsh and bamboo and tamarisk, with scatterings of wild Michaelmas daisy.

Torcello in the thirteenth century had a population of about 20,000 but 'the rivalry of Venice and the malaria due to the marshes' brought about its downfall. Its population today is about one hundred persons. Ruskin climbed to the top of the campanile and in *The Stones of Venice* rhapsodized about the view, with its 'waste of wild sea moor'.

I can overcome my general aversion to Ruskin sufficiently to acknowledge that 'wild sea moor' is a good description of Torcello. Less poetically it could be described simply as a small marshy island at the north of the Venetian lagoon, to which people come from Venice to eat at the Harry's Bar place, the Locanda Cipriani. The place, long and low beside the grassy verge of the road, and covered in creepers, has a deceptively simple *trattoria* appearance; it is, of course, expensive and smart, and much patronized by American tourists. It is also an hotel, and had plumbing long before the rest of Torcello had running water – which it now has, piped in from the mainland.

Robin McDouall, in an article about Cipriani in the *Daily Telegraph Magazine* (February 15, 1974) says that Hemingway wrote *Across the river and into the trees* at the Locanda. Cipriani, he tells me, was his authority for this statement. That Hemingway spent some time at the Locanda is not in dispute, any more than that he stayed for some time at the Gritti and worked on the novel there, as I have recounted earlier. It is possible – would seem likely – that he worked on the novel in both places, in Venice at the Gritti, and on Torcello at the Locanda. The American colonel hero of the novel returns to Venice to go duck-shooting in the lagoon, among the reedy islands, but his romance with the lovely young contessa is Venice and the Gritti, not Torcello and the Locanda, which form the background of this bit of romance-fiction.

Apart from the hotel, Torcello is a derelict place, a desolate swamp, and people come across the lagoon from Venice for the mosaics in the cathedral and the good food at the Locanda. Though, to be sure, there was a foreign lady came and bought a decaying house and a neglected vineyard, and wrote a book about it,* how she rebuilt the house and rehabilitated the vineyard, and she writes about 'our fishermen', and 'our occupations', as though she was a a born and bred Torcellan, but it would seem that she comes and goes between Paris, London and Venice in what she calls a 'triangular life'. She is very snooty about the tourists to the island, who in summer 'plod along the canal to visit the basilica, and then back again to catch the excursion boat to Venice'. What does she expect them to do – spend the night, or a week, expensively at the Locanda?

Liking 'the waters and the wild' as I do, after my seventeen years of association with Connemara, where I had a cottage, I felt I should have liked Torcello, responded to its remoteness, its lostness, its dereliction – should have been able to wax lyrical as Ruskin did, and James Morris with his 'haunted waterways'. But in truth I found it a dreary bit of swamp, and the thought of anyone living there through the winter, with not even a tourist being photographed in the Throne of Attila in the piazza to enliven the day,

* *No Magic Eden*, by Shirley Guiton, 1972.

fills me with horror. There are some twenty-six houses on Torcello, and no shops – not even a village stores; the nearest shopping place is Burano. It is only just across the water, to be sure, but you cannot walk to it, and not much of a place when you get there. Venice is six miles away across the lagoon.

The Official Guide, however, achieves the loftiest lyricism. The island is described as 'a poem of stone and water', and, it is asserted, 'he who sets foot on Torcello feels he treads on sacred land ... The lonely island of Torcello, standing out amid the languid blue of the lagoon with its square bell tower and the imposing mass of its cathedral, has many glorious pages of history in its annals.' It goes on and on like that for page after page, and concludes its Historical Notes with a poetic flourish: 'Now Torcello with its surviving monuments clustering in the small compass of the grassy square exercises an irresistible fascination over souls arthirst [*sic*] for peace. The deafening tumult of the modern world has not yet violated the magical paradise of this strip of earth. And here, in blessed solitude, amid blue and green, the spirit delights.'

How magical a paradise depends on how much marshland and lostness and desolation appeal, but Torcello is worth visiting for the golden mosaics in the cathedral, and in particular the tall, sad blue-robed Madonna holding the Child, a truly wonderful expression of Byzantine art.

Above: Venice, the Campanile and the Piazzetta; 'the campanile tipped with a tall gold angel.'

Below: The Bridge of Sighs: 'across which prisoners were taken from the prison at one side of the canal to face the State Inquisitors in the palace at the other.'

Venice, another aspect: 'decaying old houses rotting with their feet in the water.'

16
ON THE GIUDECCA

WHEN you stand on the Molo you look straight across the water to a grandiose Palladian church which appears to have an island all to itself, but it in fact shares the site with what was a Benedictine Monastery, now the Fondazione Giorgio Cini, an international centre of art and culture, with a cloister and refectory by Palladio, and an open-air theatre which is part of the Foundation.

The church is the San Giorgio Maggiore, which is also the name of the island, and it sits out there in the lagoon altogether too pompously for my taste, with its massive dome and great pillared portico, a kind of offshore island of the long, narrow strip that is the Giudecca. Henry James seems to have had reservations about it, for writing in *Portraits and Places* he says of it that it has 'success beyond all reason', adding 'it is a success of position, of colour, of the immense detached campanile tipped with a tall gold angel. I know not whether it is because San Giorgio is so grandly conspicuous, with a great deal of worn, faded-looking brickwork, but for many persons the whole place has a kind of suffusion of rosiness'.

It is anyhow easily reached from the Molo, by gondola or *motoscafo*, and between nine and twelve and three and five you can ascend the campanile by lift for 'an extensive and characteristic view of Venice, the Lagoon, the Adriatic, the Euganean Hills, and the distant Alps'. The campanile is late eighteenth century, and was designed on the lines of St Mark's. The Foundation may only be visited by writing or telephoning the Secretary in advance.

The history of the Foundation is interesting. The first church on the island was built in the late eighth century, and two centuries later the Benedictine monastery was built beside it, but both church and

K

monastery were destroyed by earthquake in 1223. The monastery was rebuilt, and in 1443 the exiled Cosimo de'Medici was its guest, and in 1799–1800 the Conclave elected Pope Pius VII there – its 'brief moment of Papal glory', as Hugh Honour calls it. But by then Napoleon had already ceded Venice to Austria, and the Austrian military used the monastery as a barracks, and for a hundred and fifty years the monastery, with Palladio's refectory – built in 1560, his earliest work in Venice – and his cloister, begun in 1579 and finished in 1614 were in a state of desuetude.

Then in 1951 Count Vittorio Cini came to its rescue; the monastery was restored and given a new life as the Fondazione Giorgio Cini, devoted to the study of Venetian civilization, and named after Count Cini's son, who was killed in an air crash. The open-air theatre, the Teatro Verde, all marble seats and cypresses, was created, for the performance of plays and operas in the summer months.

The church, on tenth-century foundations, was rebuilt by Palladio, though not completed by him. The interior is large and light and airy – and cold. Hugh Honour calls it a 'scholarly church'. It contains paintings by Bassano and Tintoretto. There are pillars and statues, and an early fifteenth-century carved wooden crucifix. Hugh Honour says, 'Every detail of decoration forms an essential part of a single plan of logical clarity. And, of course, every measurement is determined by a system of proportions.' Perhaps, after all, Ruskin was right in his detestation of Palladio.

Across a waterway called the Canale della Grazia, there is the eastern tip of the spine-like island of La Giudecca – which is, in fact, eight small islands linked by bridges. It was originally called Spinalunga, from its shape; the Blue Guide suggests that it perhaps owes its present name to the Jews of Venice, who were obliged to reside there at one time. It adds that later on it was the site of aristocratic villas and pleasure gardens, and that its most interesting building is the Franciscan church of the Redentore, 'the most complete and the most typical of Palladio's churches', and, according to Hugh

Honour, one of his greatest masterpieces. It was built, like the Salute to commemorate Venice's deliverance from the plague.

It was for this church that despite being, truth to tell, a little weary of churches by then I crossed to the Giudecca the day after my first visit to Torcello; I went not out of interest in one more Palladian church but simply to light a candle for St Francis – out of gratitude to the good Franciscan father who had gone out of his way to direct me that evening I was so hopelessly lost. Coming from a total unbeliever it was, I suppose, a highly sentimental gesture, but I am of those who think that sometimes a gesture is called for – a token offering of gratitude of support – when nothing else is possible. The good Franciscan who had helped me would know nothing of it, but it was not important that he should; what was important was that I should make the gesture – important to me, that is to say. (Well, it makes sense to you or it doesn't; to me it made sense.)

To reach the Giudecca you can take the *vaporetto* from the Schiavoni, near the Ponte del Vin, or you can walk to the Zattere, over the Accademia bridge, as I did, and take the *vaporetto* from there to the Gesuati stop.

If you are going from the Gesuati stop it is worth looking in at the church, for the Tiepolo ceiling and a Tintoretto *Crucifixion*. It is the church of Santa Maria del Rosario, and Hugh Honour says that if you leave the church by the main door, turn right, and right again along the Fondamenta Nani, 'you will see on the other side of the *rio* one of the most picturesque scenes in all Venice . . . a *squero*, one of the few remaining yards where gondolas, *sandali*, and other craft are built and repaired by traditional methods'.

On the *vaporetto* there was a young Franciscan, and when we arrived at the Giudecca I followed him to the Redentore.

I had thought that a Franciscan church would be simple, but the Redentore is austere rather than simple. It is Palladian, and high and vast and cold – 'an antiseptic fane that nobody loves', James Morris calls it. In the first chapel, on the left, as you go in, there is Tintoretto's *Ascension*, but the morning I was there it was too dark to see it properly. Somewhere near the high altar I put 100 lire into a box and took a tall candle and lit it. There were a few guttered-down candles burning, but this was the only newly lit one, and it stood out, valiantly, in the gloom, a small, flickering flame of grati-tude. I looked back at it, affectionately, from the doorway when I left. Burn, tall thin little candle, my tiny gesture. All very sentimen-tal, but I was glad to have done it – the first candle I have ever lit in a church, and probably the last. I cannot say, 'Lord, I believe,' but only, 'Help Thou my unbelief!'

Ruskin had no use at all for the Redentore; he dismissed it as 'small and contemptible, on a suburban island'. Small it is not, and 'suburban' does not, somehow, seem the right word for the Giudecca with its quaysides and handsome old houses. But Ruskin regarded the church of San Giorgio Maggiore, also, as contemptible – and gross, barbarous, childish and 'servile in plagiarism', into the bargain.

If you walk on beyond the Redentore, along the *fondamenta*, you come to the Naval Station at the end, and find yourself im-mediately opposite St Mark's, across the water. I had not realized that the Giudecca extended so far beyond the Salute, and found a shock of pleasure in the unexpected lovely confrontation.

I liked it over there on the Giudecca; the air was fresh, and there were no tourists – and none on the *vaporetto* coming over. The sun shone and the water was bright, and there were cargo boats and small naval vessels, and presently I came to a fruit and vegetable market, and beyond it a housing estate of modern blocks of flats – not high – with washing hanging from the windows between the blocks, and children played on the grass, and it was all pleasantly alive and real. Later I found a shop with the splendid name of Serafino Romeo inscribed above it.

It is hard to realize now that the Giudecca was once a garden island, a green refuge from the city of Venice. Michelangelo, exiled from Florence, lived there for a while, and Alfred de Musset declared that he wanted to spend the rest of his life there. There are still gardens there, but private and enclosed, and Hugh Honour records that the largest of them is the Garden of Eden, so called because it was laid out by an Englishman called Eden, and that opposite it stands the Palazzo Munster in which Corvo was so desperately ill with pneumonia that he received the Last Sacraments – though he recovered and lived for another three years in Venice, dying there in October, 1913. In 1910 the Palazzo Munster was the British Hospital, founded by Dr van Someren and run by Lady Layard – wife of the archaeologist – whom Corvo so relentlessly pilloried in his brilliant posthumously published novel, *The Desire and Pursuit of the Whole*, which he subtitled, 'A Romance of Modern Venice'. Corvo says that the house was formerly the summer palace of the Cornaro, but became known as the Casa del Papa, because Pope Pius VII stayed there after his election on the neighbouring islet of Sanzorzi. The house was originally a country villa on the green island of Spinalunga – the Giudecca. Corvo described 'quaint old low-pitched spacious rooms', and the hospital as 'founded by a committee of aliens resident in Venice . . . mild old darlings anxious to be charitable at the expense of a reputation for veridiction'. He calls the house the Palazza Cornaro.

Frederick Rolfe, self-styled Baron Corvo – though he claimed Papal authority for the title – had gone to Venice in the summer of 1908, on holiday with a friend, Professor R. M. Dawkins; when at the end of six weeks Professor Dawkins returned to England Rolfe stayed on – blandly ignoring his mounting bill at the hotel – a small hotel (which no longer exists) called the Belle Vue, under the clock in the Piazza San Marco. He first met Mrs van Someren early in 1909 at the Fenice Theatre, at which he was the guest of some mutual friends, Canon and Mrs Lonsdale Ragg. She did not see him again until June, when he called on her husband and told him he was homeless, having been evicted from the hotel, and that he was destitute and starving – all of which was true. Dr van Someren, well-known in Venice for his Christian charity, took Rolfe into his home, the Palazzo Mocenigo Corner on the Grand Canal. Here Rolfe had a first-floor room, and here he lived for eight months as the guest of the van Somerens, living as one of the family, and here he worked on *The Desire and Pursuit of the Whole*. Dr van Someren gave him weekly pocket money for stamps and tobacco. Rolfe was not, of course, grateful. It was the curse of his nature that he bit every hand that fed him. He complained bitterly in letters of living and sleeping 'in the open landing of a stair in this barrack of a palace'.

In another letter he described it as an 'open landing of a servant's stair' – though Mrs van Someren told Victor Hall* that it was a small room on a first-floor landing, 'unheated in winter except for a small paraffin stove, but which for the remainder of the year was pleasant enough, having a large window overlooking the adjoining garden'. He took his meals with the family, but when there were guests remained in his room, at his own request, and a tray was sent up to him. But he complained about the 'poor table' kept by the van Somerens. He 'earned his keep' by chopping wood for the domestic boiler, and working a cream separator. This, in a letter to Professor Dawkins, he described as 'chopping and carrying firewood and doing a fattorini's job'. He was very, very sorry for himself, and always smouldering with rage and resentment; but it was pathological, and he was to be pitied. But, in my view, to be admired also, for his amazing capacity for survival, and the way in which he unremittingly went on writing with all the odds stacked against him.

Young Mrs van Someren frequently inquired about the book he was so industriously working on, and begged to be allowed to read some of it; he told her she must wait until it was published, but finally he made the mistake of capitulating, and gave her the unfinished manuscript to read, but requested that she would say nothing to her husband about the work. She read at first with interest this 'Romance of Modern Venice', as he sub-titled the novel, but when she reached the uncomplimentary description of the Cosmopolitan Hospital, founded by her husband, she was highly incensed; there were also many libellous caricatures of her friends, Lady Layard, Canon Ragg, Horatio Brown, and others of the

*In an interview reported in *New Quests for Corvo*, by Cecil Woolf and Brocard Sewell, 1961.

English colony. She told Rolfe that she must withdraw her promise to say nothing of the work to her husband, and when he returned home that evening she 'informed him of the contents of the manuscript'. With the result that the doctor promptly, in turn, informed the author that he must either abandon the manuscript or leave the house. Rolfe left the Palazzo Mocenigo in the morning and went to the Bucintoro Rowing Club, where he rested by day and slept in one of the boats by night. He was once more destitute and homeless and starving. He contracted pneumonia, from exposure and undernourishment and was taken to the English hospital he had derided in his book as 'an amateurish hen-roost'.

After his remarkable recovery he, astonishingly, returned to the Belle Vue Hotel. A. J. A. Symons, in his celebrated biography, *The Quest for Corvo*, admits to being somewhat at a loss to account for this, but believes that whilst Rolfe was ill a subscription was got up by the English community for his return to England when he was well enough to travel, and that he 'accepted the surplus cash but declined the railway ticket'.

Back at the Belle Vue, in what he described as a dark, rat-infested den, he resumed work on his book, and awaited the next benefactor. This was the Reverend Justus Stephen Serjeant (whom Symons calls the Reverend Stephen Justin) and through him Rolfe was able to take an apartment in the Palazzo Marcello on the Grand Canal, early in 1913. He died there in October. The Palazzo Marcello was his final fling; he hung the walls with scarlet brocade, and had Mrs van Someren's maid make curtains from the same material – and several pyjama suits of scarlet satin. He acquired a small dog with which he walked in the Merceria, the dog wearing a scarlet bow, and the master flaunting hennaed hair. He acquired, also, a gondola, with painted sails, and manned by four gondoliers . . . a privilege usually reserved for royalty. He, who had been near to death from exposure and starvation, became the talk of Venice by his extravagance.

This 'St Martin's Summer of prosperity', as A. J. Symons called it, didn't last, for the simple reason that Justin's funds gave out; he had parted with more than £1000, Symons tells us, and 'not a penny was recouped from Rolfe's books'. Rolfe's last letter to Justin was a shameless hard-luck story of living in his boat, exposed to the elements and voracious rats, but 'prepared to persevere to the end', whereas in fact he still had the apartment in the Palazzo Marcello, which he shared with his friend Wade-Browne. In this letter he said that 'meanwhile' – meaning pending receiving another cheque – he was 'running a tick at the Cavaletto, simply that I may eat and sleep to write hard at restoring the 300-odd pages of *Hubert's Arthur* – lost in a gale in the lagoon, he had written Justin – and when that was done, he declared, he would send the manuscript, but meanwhile he was 'so awfully lonely. And tired. Is there no chance of setting me straight?'

Lonely and tired, and pretty desperate, he almost certainly was, but not starving; he was still dining at the Cavaletto, and he did so, with Wade-Browne, the night he died. Death, as Symons observes, 'superseded Mr Justin as Frederick Rolfe's last benefactor'.

He was spared another illness; he died suddenly, of heart failure; he was found by Wade-Browne, on the Sunday afternoon following their Saturday-night dinner together at the Cavaletto, lying on his bed fully dressed – Wade-Browne had called to him earlier, but receiving no answer had assumed he was still asleep. The English doctor who was summoned certified that the cause of death was in all probability heart failure, and the English Consul wrote to Rolfe's brother that 'this diagnosis was subsequently confirmed'.

Victor Hall wrote, in *New Quests for Corvo*: 'Homeless so often in life he [Frederick Rolfe] sleeps at peace at last, in a *loculus* set high in a wall of the island cemetery of San Michele, overlooking the Venice which, it may truly be said, cost him his life.'

Venice is for me very much associated with this brilliant, tragic, impossible, unhappy man, but I had not expected to meet his shade on the Giudecca.

But to return to this pleasant and interesting 'offshore island' of Venice, it is easily possible to combine a visit to the islet of San Giorgio Maggiore with a visit to the Giudecca, for there is a frequent service of *motoscafi* between the two. It is also worth noting that on the third Sunday in July there takes place the Festival of the Redentore, with attendance at the church in the morning and afternoon, and fireworks in the evening – the great feast of the Redemption. 'Everyone who has a boat – gondola, sandolo, barge or motorboat,' says Hugh Honour, 'spends the night on the water, feasting on mulberries (called *mori del Redentore*) and usually rowing over to the Lido to await the dawn.'

James Morris speaks of 'starlight concerts in the courtyard of the Doges' Palace, and band performances in the Piazza'. Corvo, in *The Desire and Pursuit*, wrote of 'the long bridge of barges across the wide canal of Zuecca' for the 'Festival of The Redentore', with 'all Venice on the water feasting in illuminated barks'. This bridge of boats across the Giudecca Canal to the church of the Redemption was in the old days for the Doge and Signoria to pass in stately procession.

It should be mentioned that there is another Palladian church on the Giudecca – the small church of Le Zitelle, meaning the Virgins, and nearby is a convent where the nuns make fine lace.

At the other side of the Giudecca Canal it is a pleasant walk along the waterfront – the *fondamenta* – of the Zattere, one way to the church of the Salute, the other way to the church of the Gesuati; either way you must cross the Accademia bridge to return to San Marco. Along the Zattere there are small shops selling Murano glass – the usual rather trashy things – roofed-over waterside cafés, blue water, a street with trees down the middle, children bounding out of school, and cats basking in the sun, or weaving around hopefully wherever humans sit at tables.

If the 1974 municipal scheme for the 'redevelopment' of Venice materializes the view from the Zattere may well be a good deal less attractive, for the Giudecca is one of the scheduled areas 'where new buildings are planned on empty sites'. This should not greatly affect the view from the Molo, as the redevelopment – always a sinister word – would appear to be concentrated towards the west, and the western tip is already a rubbish dump. New buildings will not be more than six storeys in height – otherwise, one imagines, the long thin spine that is the island of Giudecca would sink like a stone under the weight.

The city fathers' plan for the redevelopment of the city, revealed by the *Sunday Times* (February 3, 1974), who came by a copy of it, divides the city into two zones, A and B. A is the 'area of historical and environmental value', that is to say the San Marco area, and Zone B, which is the perimeter of Zone A, is the Giudecca, the already hideous area of the Piazzale Roma, with the 'bus terminal and the multi-storey garage, and the rather dreary Fondamenta Nuove to the north. The conservationists' fear that the redevelopment at the perimeter of the city will 'threaten the classical skyline', and that the 'historic heart of Venice' will become a 'warren of hotels, pensions and expensive apartments'. At present it is a warren of hotels, *pensiones* and slums, and I wonder whether the people moved out of the decaying houses of this historic heart of Venice would *want* to go back even if they could afford to. For one thing, on the mainland the *terra* is a good deal more *firma* – apart from the fact that it is where the work is.

17
THE PALAZZO REZZONICO

THE eleventh of October was my last day in Venice; it was also my seventy-third birthday. I did not mention to anyone that it was my birthday – there was, in fact, no one to mention it to – and it was just bad luck that the friend who had hoped to be in Venice on that day had not been able to 'make it'; but there were cards and letters from England, and it was all right – I was where I wanted to be on October 11, 1973.

On that day in 1963 I was aboard the dirty little Sudanese steamer that came up from Wadi Halfa, on the way to Aswan. With an English woman journalist friend living and working in Cairo I had been in the Nubian villages, wishing to see them before the waters of the Nile closed over, to become Lake Nasser, the Nubian sacrifice to the Aswan Dam. In these villages, in the Tropic of Cancer, the only water was the Nile, which, in a temperature of 120°F, you drink neat without the slightest compunction, thankful only that it is wet. We were both very unwell, with a degree of dehydration, with no saliva – which, with the tongue swollen, makes speech difficult – and no sweat and almost no urine. Additionally I had amoebic dysentery – not from drinking neat Nile, a Cairo doctor told me, but from the flies, which carry the amoebae. Of all this I wrote in *Aspects of Egypt;** that had been what I came to think of as the Nubian nightmare; this, ten years later, was the Italian journey, and the scene was Venice. On October 11, 1963, exhaustedly sipping warm beer in that dreadful little steamer, it would have been otiose to have mentioned to my equally exhausted companion that it was my birthday; all that

* 1964.

mattered then was to survive that day and night and reach Aswan, and a hotel with air-conditioning – escape from the furnace outside.

Ten years later in Venice it was nothing of a birthday, as birthdays go, since I was alone, but I had set my heart on having it there, and this was it. I was leaving for Milan and the night-train to Calais in the afternoon, but there was a whole, shining, golden morning on hand, and it seemed a pleasant idea to devote it to the Palazzo Rezzonico and the memory of Robert Browning – a poet who speaks to my condition now in the seventies as in the thirties.

As always I plotted a course with the map and the Blue Guide. The Ca' Rezzonico was not, it seemed, far from the Accademia bridge, along the canal after crossing the bridge, then over a couple of small canals to the Campo San Barnaba, with the church of that name, and you were there. A pleasant morning dander, in fact.

I left the hotel at nine and reached the Rezzonico by nine-thirty – only to discover that it was not open until ten. Well, in Italy one need never be at a loss; there is always a church at hand in which to while away time. I went into St Barnaba, which is unremarkable, just one more huge, impersonal Italian church – except for a pleasant painted ceiling, and a Veronese Holy Family in a side chapel, and it was cold and empty.

I came out of the church, glad to be out again in the warm sunshine, and strolled on the *campo*, which was arid, as *campos* tend to be, such wide open spaces as they are, with the usual well-head in the middle, the usual newspaper kiosk, and pigeons, but flanked by small shops and a café-restaurant – there was an *alimentari* with a good display of wines and cheeses, biscuits and cakes, and loaves long or flat and round. There was a butcher's offering scrawny little chickens for 990 lire, and a florist's with long-stemmed roses, and hyacinth bulbs from Holland. A newspaper poster announced that the Israelis had raided Damascus. . . .

I returned to the small canal beside the Rezzonico and hung about. There was a busyness of vegetable and wine barges, and a garbage barge with black plastic sacks stuffed full and waiting to be dumped somewhere out in the lagoon – off the Giudecca, probably, at the far end, at the Sacca Fisola, where nobody goes and nobody cares. (The garbage is used for the creation of new artificial islands.) Corvo, writing in 1909, has something to say about this in *The Desire and Pursuit of the Whole*. He makes 'Crabbe' spend much time on the new islet 'built on the lagoon mud between the islet of Santalena and the Public Gardens'. He wrote that 'the adding of fresh islets to the hundred and eighteen which compose Venice goes on slowly though surely. Recent mud-banks are staked off with double rows of massive wooden piles well rammed down: the space between is filled with concrete, and a stone wall built on the sea-face: the enclosed mud-bank is then pumped dry, and filled with rubbish stamped to a certain degree of solidity.' He speaks of a modern iron-foundry having been built on the islet of Sant'Elena, made out of the old church and monastery, but which failed financially, leaving the place deserted but for a caretaker.

Whilst we are hanging about, awaiting admission, we might as well swat up the guide books and view the Rezzonico from the outside. Hugh Honour considers it 'of all the many magnificent palaces on the Grand Canal one of the richest both outside and in'. Its history is interesting: it was designed for the Bon family in the 1660s by Longhena, but he died before it had risen above the first floor, and when in the eighteenth century the Bon family fell into financial difficulties they sold the unfinished building to the Rezzonico family – newly rich, and, says Hugh Honour, 'better able to support this *folie de grandeur*'. The Rezzonico commissioned Giorgio Massari to complete the building 'and employed the best artists to complete the interior'. They were bankers, and could afford to.

You cannot really see the Ca' Rezzonico by peering round the corner from the side canal; it can only be viewed properly from the water or from the other side of the Grand Canal. To my mind it is not really one of the handsomer of the palaces on the Grand Canal – it is too solid and square and grand. Venetian palatial beauty is the Ca' d'Oro. But Browning, whose son, Pen, bought it, thought it, 'on the whole, the best palace in Venice'. In February, 1889, the year in which, in December, he died, he wrote to George Barrett that the old Venetian families were happy that his son had bought it, so that it had 'fallen into reverent hands – not being destined to vile uses, turned into an hotel, or the like'. He was very happy to go and stay there with his son and his daughter-in-law, in October, when the various repairs had been completed. He had been staying with Mrs Bronson, at La Mura, in Asolo, and Pen, his son, brought him to the Ca' Rezzonico on October 30. He had a room on the mezzanine floor, looking along the canal to the Accademia bridge; he wrote and he read, and walked about, and had many visitors.

A room has been preserved, arranged as when he occupied it, and it was this I had gone forth to see, a pilgrimage designed as my own private birthday celebration, on October 11, 1973.

On the stroke of ten, with various Italian visitors who had by then arrived, I marched in through a gate in a courtyard, and across the courtyard and into a vast, pillared entrance hall – and marvelled that anyone should be able to think of anything so grand as 'home'.

I had noticed that the museum, on the left as you go in, up a flight of stairs, was closed. When I paid my 100 lire to the official who sat behind a counter stacked with postcards, I inquired for the Robert Browning room, and was told, to my dismay, 'Robert Browning room closed.' It was closed, like the museum, for 'restorations'. All that was available for inspection was that part of the first floor which was not the museum.

The available rooms were huge – very high, very dark; they were massively furnished and hung with enormous chandeliers; there were dark, heavily framed life-size portraits in oil, and a great deal of dark, heavy bric-à-brac. All that is of interest is in the museum, which contains the city's collection of eighteenth-century art, and there are frescoes by Tiepolo, and there is a painted ceiling and a chapel, and the rooms are furnished and decorated with an eighteenth-century elegance.

But that the museum was closed mattered less to me than that the Robert Browning room was. I tried, not very successfully, to console myself with the thought that I had anyhow made the effort, and thereby paid tribute.

Richard Church made the pilgrimage on December 12, 1949, the sixtieth anniversary of Browning's death. Venice, then, lay under snow and was swept by bitter winds, but the poet in Church – and the visionary – impelled him forth. He walked, as I did, across the Accademia bridge and over the two small canals 'and at last came to the Rezzonico'. No one was about when he arrived, and he stamped the snow from his boots and went in, walking, he writes,* along great tiled floors, 'then down to a mezzanine floor hardly above water-level, along several corridors'.

Coming, then, into the room which Robert Browning had inhabited for about six weeks, Richard Church was seized of a fantasy in which he saw Browning standing at a low window in the corner of the room, 'resting one foot up on the panelled sill, while he examined a cigar which he was about to top with a little knife set with mother-of-pearl'. The poet looked up as Church entered and declared that he was expecting a caller, that today was important, as he had a bag to pack. Then he spoke of life and death and love, quoting from his own verses, and 'the snow fell like a net curtain across the Grand Canal, flapping, against the palaces at the other side . . .' until the illusion faded, and all that was left was the room preserved as a monument, and outside the bitter wind, and Venice under snow.

During that final spell in Venice Browning was very happy, delighting in everything in the palace, marvelling at all that Pen had achieved in restoring the old place, and enjoying his routine of writing and reading and making daily trips to the Lido. (Why the Lido, one wonders; what was the fascination? Did he perhaps like the open sea at the far side?) All Venice – in terms of the English community – called on him, including the Layards. He was correct-

*In an essay entitled, 'An Encounter in Venice', in a book of essays, *Small Moments*, 1957.

ing the proofs of his *Asolando* poems, and gave readings from the work. At the end of November the weather was foggy and cold but he continued his daily excursions to the Lido, and though he developed a cough refused to see a doctor, declaring that they were all fools, and that anyhow he never caught a cold. He nevertheless developed bronchitis. He stubbornly persisted in going to a performance of *Carmen* at the Fenice, but collapsed on his return and a doctor was called . . . and warned that the danger would be his heart.

His daughter-in-law insisted on moving him from the mezzanine room to her own room, 'the sunniest in the palace', and there he continued to hold court, unaware of the gravity of his condition.

On the day on which he died he was shown a first edition copy of *Asolando*, just published and was pleased with the production, commenting on the 'pretty colour' of the binding. In the evening a telegram came from the publishers to tell him that the edition was already sold out. When Pen read him the news he declared himself 'more than satisfied', adding that he was dying. 'My dear boy,' he murmured. 'My dear boy . . .' His son, in whose face he saw his wife's, his beloved Ba, was very dear to him.

He died at ten o'clock that night, his heart finally giving out. He was seventy-seven years old. *Asolando* was his swan-song, though he had been planning additions to it.

He was not buried in Venice, though his body was taken to the cemetery of San Michele to lie in state, that Venice might pay its respects, before being taken to England for interment in the Poets' Corner of Westminster Abbey. But on the walls of the Rezzonico Palace there is inscribed in his own words his love for Italy:

> '*Open my heart and you will see*
> *Graved inside of it, "Italy".*'

18
LAST CAMPARI IN
VENICE

BACK across the Accademia bridge to the wide open spaces of the plebeian Campo Morosini – plebeian in the sense that the Piazza San Marco is patrician, that is to say – and the pleasant feeling of home-coming I always had on this square, I suppose because there I knew where I was, on trips back from the Rialto, and from forays on the Left Bank. It is helpfully signposted: *per Ponte del Accademia; per Rialto; per San Marco*; all very plain and simple; in the middle, on a plinth, stands an unremarkable statue of Nicolò Tommaseo, in a frock-coat; he was a writer, a revolutionary, and a patriot, and he deserved better than this, but from the tourist point of view it anyhow makes a change from Garibaldi.

In the Campo Morosini there are never many tourists, however, and not all that many pigeons, but numerous children, racing about, jumping from steps, cycling, or engrossed in doing mysterious things with chalk on the paving stones. There is a greengrocer's shop on the corner of the lane that leads through per San Marco, with a fine outside display of fruit and vegetables; there are unimportant, unsmart cafés, lamp standards quite as handsome as those on San Marco, and two churches, the Gothic San Stefano at one end, and the Palladian San Vitale at the other. I offer no apologies or excuses for not going into either; whenever I was on the Campo Morosini, which was often, I was either going somewhere, or returning from somewhere; but for those interested, the San Vitale is a disused church, and admittance is through the art gallery next door. Inside there is a Carpaccio painting of St Vitalis riding one of the bronze horses of San Marco, and some eighteenth-century

L

sculpture. San Stefano has a leaning tower and Tintorettos, and
Francesco Morosini is buried therein. And if you ask who was Francesco Morosini that he should be buried in a church and have a square
named after him I can only tell you that he fought the Turks in
the middle and late seventeenth century, that he was elected Doge
in 1688, and fought the Turks for the fourth time in 1693, in charge
of the Venetian forces ... and it is said that so great was the terror
of his name that the enemy withdrew at the mention of it. Why
Nicolò Tommaseo stands in the middle of the Campo Morosini
and not Francesco himself can only be explained in terms of 'honours
even', though I am personally prejudiced on the side of Tommaseo,
because he was a writer, and went on writing until the end, even
though in his last years he had lost his sight.

Anyhow, there I was back in the Campo Francesco Morosini
after my frustrated attempt to see the Robert Browning room in
the Palazzo Rezzonico on my birthday, and my last day in Venice,
and with a few hours still in hand before I need step into the motor-
launch for the hateful Piazzale Roma and the railway station and the
train for Milan, I was – it being near midday – looking for the last
Campari. Hugh Honour says, and I agree with him, that when you
are tired of the grandeurs and the tourists of the Piazza San Marco
'you cannot choose a better place to drink your *aperitivo* or coffee
than the Campo Morosini', which he likes, as I do, for its ordinariness
and its children. But for me the Campo Morosini is a place of transit,
coming or going, not for loitering, and I continued on through the
narrow lanes to the wider thoroughfare of the Calle Larga XXII
Marzo, one of the widest streets in Venice, and commemorating
the day on which the Venetians expelled the Austrians, in 1848.
If you continue along this street you come to the florid 'grotesque
baroque' church of San Moisè, which Ruskin declared was 'one of
the basest examples of the basest school of the Renaissance'; if you
continue on from there you come to San Marco; if you turn left
before you come to the church you reach the Fenice Theatre, and
if you turn right at the canal, just before the church, you come into
narrow alleyways, and the tucked-away little Pensione Budapest,

and so to the creeper-covered courtyard of the back entrance of the Europa.

The Calle Largo XXII Marzo is pleasant to stroll in because it is wide enough for comfort, and is a thoroughfare, not just a claustrophobic dark lane or alleyway. It has banks, travel agencies, and shops assorted. Hugh Honour says that No. 2251 is the agent 'for the Fortuny silks so highly praised by Proust', adding that they are 'made in a factory of the Giudecca and frequently repeat the patterns of textiles in paintings by Veronese and Tiepolo'.

I had my last Campari in a small snack-bar place on the Calle Largo XXII Marzo, munching a small sandwich at the bar, then continued on to San Moisè, for the façade of which, says Hugh Honour, 'no one has ever had a good word'. The Blue Guide describes its façade as 'overcharged', and James Morris refers to it as a Baroque extravaganza, and says that it 'usually stops the tourists in their tracks, so laughably elaborate is its façade'. It did not affect me like that; I passed it every day, coming out of the back entrance of the Europa and coming round past the Budapest and the little canal on my way to San Marco, one way, or the Accademia the other. To me it seemed just one more over-ornate Italian church, and it was just a matter of up the steps and down the steps over the small canal and on down the Salizzada San Moisè to San Marco, and the Salizzada just the usual lane of dress shops, antique shops, glass shops. I never felt attracted to the interior of the church, disliking both its florid façade and its name San Moisè Profeta, and the Blue Guide has nothing to say about it except that inside the entrance there is the grave of John Law, 1671–1729, originator of the 'Mississippi Scheme', transferred from San Geminiano in 1808. Hugh Honour, however, describes the high altar as like a rock garden, with a gargantaun piece of sculpture representing Moses receiving the tablets of the law on Mount Sinai. He speaks also of a chancel painting by Giovanni Pellegrini, 'the best of the eighteenth-century Venetian painters errant who travelled across Europe brightening walls and ceilings with southern colour'. Close by the church is the ugly modern building of the Bauer-Grunwald Hotel, as relentlessly functional, architecturally, as the church is ornate.

I might have gone into San Moisè after that last Campari but that when I had gone up the steps and down the steps over the canal I was overwhelmed by the sight of gigantic funeral wreaths outside the church, some of them supported on stands, others laid out on the ground. I have never in my life seen such enormous, such Gargantuan wreaths. One, mounted on a stand, was a mass of wine-coloured dahlias enlivened by the exotic orange, bird-like blooms of 'queen flowers'. There were massed red roses, massed pink carnations, great spikes of gladioli of all colours, huge fronds of palm, and great sashes of black ribbon. I spent so long gazing, fascinated, at these monstrous – as it seemed to me – floral tributes, and attempting to decipher the great cards that accompanied them, that after making a few notes I realized that my time had run out and that if I was not to keep the man from Sommariva waiting I must hurry, so I scurried back, up the steps and down the steps, across the little canal, and along the mini arcade beside it, and round the corner by the Pensione Budapest, and along the narrow lane to the courtyard at the back of the Hotel Europa, and then by a complication of corridors to the reception desk of the Regina, where I inquired was anyone of importance being buried that day at the church of San Moisè, that so many and such huge wreaths had been brought there. The receptionist said not that he knew of, and then picked up a local paper from under the counter and searched in its columns for news of an important funeral that day, but there was nothing that he could see.

'But such *huge* wreaths,' I insisted, and raised a hand above my head, high, to indicate the height.

He smiled and shrugged, non-committally. Then he passed an open register to me across the counter. If I would be so kind as to write my name and address, in case any letters should come after my departure.

I wrote my name and address, then after an exchange of *arrive-dercis* and *grazies* made my way back through the labyrinth and into the huge, chandelier-hung lounge of the Europa, where the Sommariva man waited at the reception desk, and a motor-launch chugged at the landing stage beyond the deep French windows on to the Grand Canal.

A good view of the Ca' Rezzonico as we hurtled past, and people were landing there from a *vaporetto.* . . .

I was glad, all the same, that I had walked to it, as Browning himself must have done, many times, across the Accademia bridge, and as Richard Church did through the snow and bitter wind on December 12, 1949, impelled by some strange necessity.

Sentimentally I should have had that last Campari on the San Marco, at Florian's, for it was there, at midday, on April 18, 1964, that I drank my first. I had arrived overnight by train from Calais, second-class, without benefit of sleeper or couchette, and after breakfasting on the railway station with the Greek girl who had driven me crazy in the night, but about whom, come morning, I no longer felt homicidal. We walked across the city to San Marco together, she constantly halting to gaze into bead shops in the narrow lanes, and arrived eventually at the Piazza, where we parted. She had some friends to meet. We would see each other again, no doubt, on the Greek steamer to Alexandria that evening. I did not, in fact, see her again, and it was no loss to either of us, for we were not for each other. She was going home to Athens, and I was en route for Cairo. When we had parted company on the Piazza San Marco I wandered for hours, renewing acquaintance with Venice after nearly forty years, as I have told elsewhere,* and finally, at noon, came to rest at Florian's, though only a handful of people sat there, because it was in the shade, whereas Quadri's, at the other side of the square, was in full sunshine, and its orchestra scraping away, and its rows of tables occupied. I was the only occupant of the front row of tables at Florian's, but it had to be Florian's for me that day – for old times' sake. At the nearest occupied table I noticed that all the glasses were filled with a pink drink, and when

* *Stories from My Life,* 1973.

the waiter came for my order I asked him what was that drink, and he replied, 'Campari-soda, signora,' That meant nothing to me, but I did not want to drink sweet Italian vermouth, and I did not feel like beer, and coffee would be for later, so I said I would have that – a Campari-soda. It came in a little bottle, the Campari ready mixed with soda, but later I learned that this was not the best way to have Campari, that one should order Campari and add soda to taste. But anyhow it came like that and it was delicious, and after that I drank Campari-sodas all the way to Alexandria, and went on drinking them in Cairo, and one day in the lounge of the old Semiramis Hotel an American woman came over to me and said to excuse her, but what was that pink drink I was drinking, and was it a *soft* drink, and I said no, it was not a soft drink, it was an Italian aperitif and it was delicious. I hope I made a convert. I drank Campari-sodas all the way to America in 1966, and all the way back again; and I drank them on this Italian journey in 1973, but at the moment of writing I am of the under-privileged who do not know there the next Campari is coming from. (Or for that matter the soda, it being one of the several current shortages.)

Anyhow, that April noon in 1964 I was initiated into the bitter-sweet pleasure of Campari, at Florian's, but nine years later I had no desire to sit at that historic café, nor at Quadri's either, for at all hours both were choc-a-bloc with tourists, mostly American, but interspersed with Germans and English, and with the babble and the crowdedness it was like nothing so much as Oxford Circus during the rush hour. In the evenings the orchestras at both cafés would be scraping away with soulful romantic stuff, the good old Italian equivalent of *schmaltz*, and the serried ranks of tourists of all nations manifestly love it, but for me it is, in good Runyonese, music the type I am not liking.

The Piazza San Marco was altogether crowded in September and October, morning, noon and evening, a little less so in October, but with the crowds still pretty dense. September was always the 'high season' in Venice, of course, and unless you enjoy crowds, or can travel at no other time, that month is best avoided. I would personally avoid October, also, and always settle for April; when I was there, mid-April, in 1964, the tourists were thin on the ground; in the autumn of 1973 I often felt almost hysterical in the density of the throng milling on the Piazza San Marco and in the Piazzetta and on the Molo. I felt at times that it was hardly to be borne! Hugh Honour says that if he were to be limited to a single annual visit to Venice he would make it October, November, April, or early May, 'thus avoiding the summer crowds and the winter weather, though unfortunately missing the pleasures of bathing, concerts, operas and regattas'. I would eliminate October, from my own experience. Hugh Honour wrote in 1965, and by 1973 *everything* had become more 'dense', tourism not least. There are, simply, more people visiting more places, and this is good, but also it calls for 'staggering' in the time-tables.

It is not only the crowds on the streets and the piazzas which are fearsome, but the liability of hotels to become inundated by 'groups'. Then the pleasantly quiet dining-room of the night before becomes transformed into a frightful overcrowded party in which a mob of human beings babble away at the tops of their voices, completely deafeningly. This cannot happen, of course, if you are staying at some small *pensione* – or at the Gritti. But it can and does happen at any first- and second-class hotel in between.

I do not think that the dream-like beauty of Venice can be properly appreciated during the high season. You must be able to *see* the Piazza and the Piazzetta, not just the tops of the buildings – wonderful though those tops are. The mosaic façade of the Basilica of St Mark's has to be approached across the Piazza for the full impact of its golden splendour. The great – and magnificent – bronze horses need to be seen uncluttered by human bodies pressing about them, and the mighty Moors of the clock tower also. The arcades that flank the Piazza lose their charm when they become as crowded as Oxford Street; they are for strolling in, past the displays of lace and glass and mosaic work. It is very pleasant to have drinks or coffees at Florian's or Quadri's when they are not crowded, and quite pointless to sit there when they are.

Once you have left the San Marco area, of course, the crowds thin out, and the further you go along the Schiavoni the fewer the people, and it is never crowded over at the Salute, or on the Giudecca and you can have the Fondamenta Nuove more or less to yourself. The last stretch of this waterfront was a favourite haunt of Corvo, and he wrote of it in *The Desire and Pursuit of the Whole*, making 'Nicholas Crabbe' wander there when he was down and out, enjoying the 'view of the cemetery-island, and the Island-City of Murano, and all the lagoon to the mainland twenty miles away and to the ridge of the Alps seventy miles away . . .' Then at dusk he would begin walking briskly 'through the populous alleys'.

He visited the cemetery island, across the bridge of boats, on the Day of the Dead, the Feast of the Redentore. Had Corvo himself any idea that he himself would eventually rest there? Since he had no intention of returning to England, or going elsewhere, one can only suppose so.

He makes Crabbe – pretty certainly himself, in this intensely autobiographical novel – spend his last few coins on 'an armful of white chrysanthemums and a handful of white rose-buds', though he had not eaten for a week, and had reached the point at which he could not so do, surviving on water sipped at a fountain, at night, on some *campo*. He laid the rose-buds at the urn containing the ashes of a cremated baby, an English baby called Lawrence, 'burned and forgotten'. The white chrysanthemums he laid at the grave of an English engineer who had died at the British Hospital, the Universal Infirmary . . . of his savage hate. He 'marked out a great white cross of chrysanthemums on the level grass', and prayed for the repose of Protestant souls, 'that they might also pray for him in his great loneliness'. The cemetery is described as a garden, in which Crabbe slowly paced along cypress avenues, 'between the graves of little children with blue or white standards and the graves of adults marked by more sombre memorials'.

I have no regrets about not visiting San Michele, and if I am ever in Venice again I still will not do so, having a profound distaste for the Cult of the Dead, but for those who enjoy cemeteries the short trip across the lagoon to this island which is nothing but – by Napoleonic decree – must undoubtedly afford an interesting excursion. James Morris has a detailed description of it in his book. He describes the cemetery as 'wide and calm, a series of huge gardens, studded with cypress trees and awful monuments'. There are hundreds of thousands of tombs, both lavish and humble, he records. There is a Protestant corner, and an Orthodox enclosure – in which lies Serge Diaghilev. High up in a tomb terrace is to be found the burial place of the mortal remains of Frederick William Serafino Austin Lewis Mary Rolfe, 'Baron Corvo'. His was most passionately, most violently and bitterly and despairingly, the desire and pursuit of the whole, but as the believer would say he was 'not given the grace'. But his end was merciful, and some of us remember him, with compassion, as we pass, and repass on the *vaporetto* the cypress-avenued island of San Michele, even though we do not go ashore.

Venice is unique, it is the 'jewel casket of the world'; it is most wonderful; but there is also a sense in which it is 'too much'; too many churches; too many palaces; too many paintings; too much culture altogether; too much for the ordinary intelligent but non-culture-hound person to cope with. I have a good deal of sympathy with the disgruntled London shop-assistant who grumbled to me that her package-tour holiday for Austria had been switched to Italy – '*Venice!*' she said bitterly. 'We've *been* to Venice!' The year before she had proudly shown me muzzy snapshots of herself and friends in gondolas, and feeding the pigeons in St Mark's Square. She had evidently enjoyed the trip, what with it being Italian, and gondolas and that. But what would you do a second time, for God's sake? In her unlettered way she has a case; wonderful as it all is there can come a point at which you have had enough . . . for the time being, anyhow. I would always like to go back to cross a few t's and dot a few i's; for one thing I have never been in the Accademia Gallery; nor seen inside the Ca' d'Oro, nor visited the little pink

and grey Renaissance church of Santa Maria Miracoli, out beyond the
Rialto. I could always use some more time in Venice, and yet when
I got back from Verona that last time I counted the days and the
hours to that last Campari. Because with any city as culturally dense
as Venice there does just come that point when enough is enough.
Yet to believe that that last-Campari-in-Venice really *was* the last
Campari-in-Venice would be a little death-in-Venice.

There are foreigners who live there and like it – though the
natives seem to try hard to get out. Did Corvo enjoy living there?
He seems to have had a love-hate relationship with it, but he had
finally settled for it and had no choice. He liked – when he did not
despise – the 'ribald, venal, dishonest, licentious young gondoliers'.
He found refuge in his homelessness in the churches, hearing Mass
after Mass. He was always intensely aware of the city's beauty; and
of its squalors. He wrote and starved and raged and suffered and
struggled, and finally died there, unfulfilled. 'Nicholas Crabbe'
eventually found the Whole, in the union of two halves that had
found each other 'and were joined and dissolved in each other as
one', but this consummation of the Desire and Pursuit was not
vouchsafed to Rolfe himself, and he died as he had lived lonely
and alone.

Yet Venice suited his temperament as no other city – except
possibly Paris – would have done; in Venice he could 'cultivate
the garden of his soul in the loneliness of sea and sky'. One way
and another it suited him.

For the random visitor it has to be, I think, taken in small doses,
a week or two at a time, preferably in the early spring, before the
international tourist crowds take over. Though, to be sure, a great
piazza like that of San Marco was designed to be a place where
people would congregate, to promenade, gossip, sit at cafés;
designed, that is, as a centre for human busyness. It is only that, in
the 'high season', it is just a little *too* busy, *too* crowded, for comfort.
And as a purely tourist note, the hotels and *pensioni* are well-heated
in the colder months, and the rates are lower out of season.

Venice is a great and wonderful museum, and I do not share the to me puritanical view that this is a degradation of a great city. Venice is not a 'great city' in the sense that London, Paris, New York are; or, in a secondary category, Rome, Milan, Naples. Venice is *unique*. I do not know what other city is so rare, unless it is the rock-hewn, rose-red Nabatean city of Petra; or Jerusalem before it was defiled by the Zionist Occupation.

There are two schools of thought, today, about Venice. There are those who are for her preservation as a wonderful museum, as James Morris puts it, 'a lovely backwater, preserved in artistic inutility, while commerce and industry should be confined to the mainland suburb of Mestre, technically part of the Municipality. The other school wishes Venice . . . to be given new meaning by an infusion of modern activities.' James Morris does not, that I can see, commit himself, either to the 'aesthetic conservers on the one hand, the men of change on the other'. He believes that 'the true purpose of Venice lies somewhere between, or perhaps beyond, the two extremes'. For myself I would settle for Venice as a museum – and thank God (or something, or someone) for one of the better facts of life.

Because, as I see it, Venice has long ceased to be a viable proposition as a *city*. Well, would *you* like to live in some handsome old, rotting old, rat-ridden palazzo without running water – just because it was Venice? Of course not. If you found yourself in that predicament you would move, at the first opportunity, across to the mainland and the amenities, even if it meant a cement block.

There are those who assert, 'Ah yes, but Venice could be *modernized*. It could be *made* into a viable city, in which people could live happily, and work, and live normal, urban lives.' It is a nice idea, but I do not, myself, believe it. Venice cannot be made a viable city, in the modern sense, without industrialization . . . and it is the pollution of industrialization from Mestre and Marghera that is already damaging the ancient monuments, and, as I write, one of the great bronze horses of the Quadriga, over the main entrance to St Mark's, has just been taken down, to be tested 'for possible corrosion'.

The younger generation of Venetians will always opt for the mainland, where the work is – and the warm, dry apartment with all the mod cons. As a waiter in Verona said to me, when I asked where he came from and he said Venice, and I asked if he preferred Verona, 'Who wants to live in Venice? It is sinking! It *is* sinking...'

As to that, it is, and it isn't.

19
VENICE IN PERIL

VENICE *is*, of course, faced with the problem of subsidence, but there is a sense in which this is the least of its problems, since it is one which can be, and in fact *is*, being coped with, whilst the problem of air and water pollution is very much more difficult to tackle; it is this pollution which is destroying Venice, and the problem it presents is enormous. Venice can be saved from sinking into the lagoon, and by camparison with the pollution problem this one is relatively simple . . . the key-word is 'relatively'.

It has been established that the main cause of subsidence is due to the excessive exploitation of the lagoon by the mainland industrial areas. A UNESCO report (September, 1972) says that the new aqueduct under construction will be completed in three or five years' time and may reduce the sinking processes. 'The storm surge mechanism and effects in the Adriatic Sea' being now understood, though information is not yet complete, it is believed that the city may be saved from floods. The most urgent of the engineering projects is the one for the regulation of the flow of water from the Adriatic into the Lagoon through the mouths of the Lido, Malamocco and Chioggia. The laboratory for research and experimental work into all this is financed by the Italian Government, and with the collaboration of UNESCO numerous internationally known scientists have been able to participate in the various investigations and projects. The Italian Government has raised, through foreign loans, over £200 million for measures to halt the subsidence of Venice, eliminate or control the sources of pollution, and for the repair of houses, monuments and works of art.

Writing in *Country Life* for May 10, 1973, Sir Ashley Clarke,

Vice-Chairman of the Venice in Peril Fund, says that 'one of the major tasks to be performed by the State is the placing of sluice-gates at the entrances to the lagoon . . . to control the onset of very high water'. He writes, also, of the problem of sewage and refuse disposal, and of the general problem of pollution. In addition to the creation of a proper sewage system there have also to be aqueducts to being fresh water from the rivers to the industrial zones, 'so that excessive use of the fresh water in the subsoil, which is probably the main reason for the sinking of Venice, can be stopped'. It is also desirable that at least some part of the industry established at Marghera, at the edge of the lagoon, should be re-sited, notably the petro-chemical installations and refineries. This would be costly and call for political courage, says Sir Ashley, 'but it should not be technically impossible to resite it on the Adriatic coast'.

On the conservation side an emormous amount has been achieved by outside private initiative, supported by the Italian authorities. The Venice in Peril Fund in London, under the chairmanship of Lord Norwich, has completed the restoration of the church of the Madonna del'Orto – Tintoretto's parish church and burial place – and is working on the Sansovino loggia at the foot of the Campanile, working always in close co-operation with UNESCO. The Federal Republic of Germany has been responsible for the restoration of Santa Maria dei Miracoli, as well as for work on paintings. The Austrian Government has made provision for the restoration of a Venetian palace which it will subsequently use as the headquarters of a cultural institute. Belgium and the Netherlands, Denmark and Sweden, have all shown an active concern for the preservation of Venice. The United States of America, through its Committee to Rescue Italian Art, set up after the 1966 flood, has made an enormous contribution. This committee is no longer in operation, being replaced by the International Fund for Monuments, whose Venice Committee began work with the restoration of the façade of the Ca' d'Oro in 1967. Another American Committee, Save Venice, Inc., established in 1970, has various restoration projects in hand. The Committee to Rescue Italian Art carried out a number of valuable restorations, including roofing work on the church of San Moisè, and the restorations of canvases and frescoes.

In 1968 a laboratory was established in the disused church of San Gregorio, and in the building next to it, for the restoration of paintings. It was established on the initiative of the Soprintendenza alle Gallerie, but it owes much to the Italian Art and Archives Rescue Fund, of which Sir Ashley Clarke was Chairman, and from which the British Committee, the Venice in Peril Fund, took over.

From all of which it will be seen that a tremendous international effort is being made to save Venice, both from subsidence and from the effects of pollution – though the sources of the pollution can only be dealt with at government level. The British Committee appeals, poignantly, to 'everyone who loves Venice, or has been happy there', to donate to its Venice in Peril Fund that it may continue its restoration work, and that it is doing a good job is evident from the work already accomplished and for those who care about the architectural and artistic splendours of Venice it is a cause worthy of support – and obviously anyone of any aesthetic sensibilities must care – but when you wander around in Venice, away from the San Marco area, going up the steps and down the steps over innumerable little bridges over innumerable dark, narrow, smelly little canals, and see the decaying old houses rotting with their feet in the water, their façades scabrous with neglect, you realize that saving Venice is not just a matter of restoring churches and flood-damaged paintings, valiant and commendable and support worthy as such efforts are, but a matter of salvaging a whole city. Away from the shining, splendid San Marco area Venice is a labyrinth of crumbling, rat-infested slums. Many of these tenements could be restored and modernized, with running-water and the basic mod cons, and utilized as decent apartments – not to be let or sold expensively to wealthy foreigners, but for ordinary middle-class and working-class Venetians, and there is in fact, such a municipal scheme. Though whether this would in fact halt the migration of the younger generation to the mainland is debatable –

the *work*, after all, is over there. Such a scheme would anyhow rehouse those at present living in the tenements, and *might* be an inducement to the young would-be escapees to stay. Certainly only such a scheme can preserve Venice as a living city – rescue it from the role d'Annunzio so fiercely resented, of being little more than a wonderful museum. Though certain risks are involved in that, and, as I said earlier, I would settle for it as a wonderful museum. Cities, like civilizations, come to an end; Nineveh lies buried – palaces and temples and villas and all – under the desert sands, and Sodom and Gomorrah lie at the bottom of the Dead Sea.

Venice need not sink into the lagoon; modern technology can, as the Americans say, take care of that – and is in fact doing so; whether, in the context of the modern world, Venice can be saved from the destroying pollution of its mainland industrialization is another matter. There are those who would drain the Grand Canal and turn it into a motorway, and drive a road from the Piazzale Roma through to the Piazza San Marco ... in the name of modernization and progress. Think what a splendid car park it would make, and the convenience to the tourists, who could drive on at the lagoon and drive off at the Lido! Not to mention the extensions of car-ferry services to the islands! You can't put the clock back, etc., and all things are possible in an age so bound and delivered-over to materialism that it can make a musical out of the life and death of Jesus of Nazareth – blasphemy, like love, is an outdated word. Finally, perhaps, it is from *entrepreneurs* that Venice has to be saved. For Venice so to be taken over would be the fate worse than death; better she should sink inviolate into the lagoon, to be remembered as an ancient dream of beauty, the jewel casket of the world, the Serene Republic, the Serenissima of a lost civilization.

20

ARRIVEDERCI

AFTER that last Campari on the Calle Largo XXII Marzo, and the inspection of the huge funeral wreaths outside the over-embellished church of San Moisè, it was a relief to be aboard the midday train to Milan – and an even greater relief to be in my compartment on the night-train to Calais. It was a relief because an hour or so before you leave a place it has already died on you; there is a sense in which you have already left it; the hotel bedroom has no longer anything to do with you – it awaits the next inmate; the hotel itself has detached itself from you – your baggage may still stand – hopelessly insignificantly – in the entrance lounge, but you have finished with the hotel and it has finished with you; you have finished with the place itself, and want now only to be gone from it; you have rejected it all, but it has even more strongly rejected you – you are no longer of the slightest interest there. Once you are aboard the train or 'plane or ship of your departure you are of a certain minor interest; you are a passenger, with a name or number; you have an identity, if only as the lawful occupant of a seat, a berth, a cabin. You are of some very slight consequence again. One day, perhaps, I might have the good fortune to return to Venice, I thought, filling in time on that last morning, but meanwhile I had finished with it – and it with me. Now, like Macbeth, or Macduff, or whoever it was, I would stand not upon the order of my going.

The train journey from Venice to Milan seemed even duller and more tedious than on the incoming journey, which was at least enlivened-by the excitement of the first glimpse of the lagoon. The first glimpse of Milan, all modern apartment blocks, does nothing at all for one. The first-class compartment was full, and the Italian bourgeoisie are as flaccid as the bourgeoisie anywhere. When a

M

girl staggered in, panting from lugging a heavy suitcase, not one of the several men in the compartment rose to help her get it up into the rack; it was left to an elderly Englishwoman to do so, and she thanked me with a charming smile and obvious gratitude. Italian men, in my observation, are in general ungallant; they never rise when their womenfolk come to their tables in a restaurant, and when a man and woman enter together the man seats himself, leaving the woman to fend for herself. If the food he has ordered comes before hers he tucks into it. In public vehicles he always takes the corner seat. The concept of good manners varies, of course, from country to country, but the Italian male, it seems to me, lacks ordinary human considerateness. There are, I am sure, Italian men with charming manners and an exquisite considerateness; I report only on what I observed on public transport, in streets, at cafés, and in the restaurants of first-class hotels.*

Vicenza again, with its clock tower and a domed building at the top of a wooded ridge; then Verona – and again I help a young woman entering the compartment with a heavy suitcase and none of the men lifting a hand. The young woman, settles in her seat and opens a magazine, on which a headline catches my eye; *Una bambina di 80 anni. Per Mae West il tempo si è fermato.* Which I take to mean that for the eighty-year-old Mae West time stands still, which is a handsome tribute.

At Milan, soon after five, I am met by the good Giovanni, who organizes me with a carrier-bag of food for the journey, there being no restaurant car on the train; it costs 1700 lire, which with only 1300 to the £ is expensive; the provisions include a veal cutlet, bread, cheese, cakes, and a quarter bottle of wine. Giovanni says that the price of a packed meal has gone up by 400 lire in the

---

*After writing this I was interested to read what Peter Nicholls, the Rome correspondent of *The Times*, for the past fifteen years, says in his book, *Italia, Italia* (1974), about the Italian male, whom he finds 'spoilt from birth' and 'infuriatingly cocksure' – convinced of his irresistibility to women, conditioned by his upbringing, and influenced by the two renowned symbols of virility, Casanova and Valentino.

last few weeks. He also says that it is announced on the public address system that the train is only going to Paris, to the Gare de Lyon, from which it will be necessary to get a taxi to the Gare du Nord, for Calais; owing to a French rail workers' dispute. But there is apparently some uncertainty as to whether there will be a train from the Gare du Nord. It will be necessary to make inquiries on the spot. Giovanni, ever helpful, makes various inquiries on my behalf, but all is uncertainty. I had looked forward to being aboard the Milan–Calais train as an end of all travel anxieties and difficulties; once safely aboard the train at Milan, in my sleeping compartment, I had told myself, I would be able to relax. An additional piece of bad news aboard the train was that there would be no *petit-déjeuner* next morning; no hot coffee with which to bind body and soul together again after the night journey.

In the corridor of the train, before we left, the young woman with whose suitcase I had helped when she had entered the compartment at Verona smiled, friendlily, and inquired, 'Are you still writing a book?'

'Well, yes,' I said, 'but how did you know?'

'I saw you on the boat to Chioggia,' she said. 'You were taking notes all the time. I thought that anyone looking about so intently and taking so many notes must be writing a book.' She added, endearingly, 'Also I read English books and newspapers and I think I have seen your picture.'

I owned up, then, and we chatted. She had spoken such fluent Italian with the Italian woman next to her in the train from Venice that I had assumed she was Italian, but she proved to be Swiss – which I suppose accounted for her equally fluent English. We agreed that we had not much cared for Chioggia and that it had been quite a business getting there. Then a ticket inspector came along and we each returned to our compartments and I never saw her again, and I became involved in conversation with a small anxious Englishwoman who complained that she didn't understand about the train not going to Calais, because it *said* Calais on the outside

of the coach; Calais and *London*, she said, and she had been told
that all she had to do was to sit in the train until it got to Calais....
She regarded me, helplessly. I explained about the French rail
dispute. I asked if she had any French francs and she said no. I
said, well, I had, and we'd need them for the taxi across Paris to
the Gare du Nord, so she had better share a taxi with me. 'But with
any luck,' I said, to cheer her up, 'the train will go on to Calais.'
She said, almost tearfully, that she did *hope* so; it did, after all,
say Calais on the outside ...

Well, anyone booked for Calais, or Heaven, or anywhere else,
nowadays ain't necessarily goin' there. I returned to my compartment and opened up the Milan bag of victuals and poured myself a
glass of wine – which proved to be red and pleasant. There would
be a scramble for taxis at the Gare de Lyon, I reflected, and the
thing would be to tack on to an English *man*, not flounder around
on my own with that helpless little Englishwoman; I wouldn't
abandon the poor thing, but a *man*, I thought, in my non-Women's-
Lib fashion, would be an asset – especially if he spoke better French
than I did, which should not be difficult.

I poured another glass of that really-quite-passable Italian red
wine – not Chianti Classico, perhaps, but entirely drinkable – and
faced the Reality of no-trains-to-Calais when the taxis set us all
down at the Gare du Nord. What then? Another taxi to the air-
terminal and a bid to get a seat on a 'plane? Or did one just pick
up one's bags at the Gare du Nord and march into the nearest hotel
and book in and relax, accepting a day or two in Paris as a kind of
bonus, and not worrying? Either way it would involve sending
wires to England, to one's nearest and dearest, concerning delayed
return. Most of us, I supposed, would try for a 'plane that day;
important would be to send the telegrams to the people who would
be expecting us, and in some instances meeting us.

I left my compartment and wandered down the corridor, vaguely
looking for someone with whom to discuss The Situation. I found
no one; everyone was closeted . . . but finally a compartment
with its door hospitably opened on to the corridor revealed the

little Englishwoman who had been so flummoxed. She sat in a corner by the door, and responded, wanly, to my smile of recognition.

'Don't worry,' I said, 'we'll get to London, somehow!'

A raw-boned-looking woman seated next to her snorted.

'I mean,' I said, defensively, 'it may never happen – the train may go through to Calais.'

This produced a retort from the raw-boned one, but I comprehended only the sense of it, not speaking the language, which was Scottish, but it was derogatory, I think, to do with Sassenachs who always feared the worst. Though, in fact, I hoped for the best. The little Englishwoman, anyhow, brightened.

Hungering and thirsting after conversation, having had very little of it throughout the Italian journey, I leaned against the doorway and lapsed into loquaciousness, confiding that it was my seventy-third birthday, and reminiscing about that day ten years ago . . . and the Scottish comment on this penetrated to my Sassenach understanding; and serve me right.

'It seems,' said the raw-boned one, 'ye shouldna travel on yair bairthday!'

I smiled, amiably.

'Looks like it,' I said, and returned to my compartment.

It was a night of very little sleep, what with the train continually stopping – threateningly, it seemed – and the over-riding anxiety.

Nevertheless, we reached Paris, at the Gare de Lyon, at the scheduled time, six-thirty – by which time we all stood dressed but unslept in the corridor, gazing out blearily at the empty station, ready to bundle out into it, if need be, and cope as best we could with the rest of the journey, hoping for the best whilst fearing the worst.

We were, however, reprieved. A train attendant came along telling us not to alight; there was a possibility that the train might go on to the Gare du Nord; even to Calais . . .

After a long delay the train went on. An hour later we were leaving the Gare du Nord, and at nine-fifteen a restaurant-car was put on. *Vive la France!*

The *petit-déjeuner* was eight francs, this time, about eighty pence – as opposed to six francs, on the way out, a few weeks ago – but it was good to have the coffee, 'instant' though it was, and most of us, I feel sure, would have paid anything within our means for that. The restaurant-car was terribly cold, but there is something about hot coffee after a night-journey on a train. . . .

France was enveloped in thick white fog, with no visibility beyond the bushes at each side of the line, but by Amiens it was clearing and presently there was sunshine. We reached Boulogne – not Calais – in bright sunshine, around eleven. We had 'made it' to the coast, and anxiety should have ended there, but in fact it didn't for we learned over the public address system when we stood with our baggage in a large embarkation hall with very little seating, that there was something amiss with the ship – some 'technical' trouble – and we were delayed for an hour.

We got into the dreary railway slum that is Victoria Station (Heavens, how scruffy and dreary is that Continental arrival area nowadays! What on earth do foreigners arriving for the first time from the Continent make of it, at all?) at five-fifteen; the friend who had seen me off and come to meet me on my return, and who had been there at three, for the three-thirty arrival, had gone away at five to get a cup of tea, being by then both cold and weary, and having been assured at the Information Office that the boat-train would not arrive until five-thirty at earliest. So thanks to that bit of British Rail inefficiency we missed each other by minutes.

I hung about for a while, then, deciding that not even the most devoted of friends who had set out to meet a train at three-thirty would still be there nearly two hours later, to meet an 'unscheduled' train, I struggled home on the Underground in the rush-hour – and struggled is the word. I was in the house within the hour, very exhausted, and so very glad to *be* there – *there* as opposed to being on a train from Milan that might or might not continue on to the French coast, or even as far as Paris, Gare du Nord. The last time I had gone to Paris, in 1971, I had run into a French rail strike, with all attendant anxiety.

But travel is always attended by hazard – which is what makes it an adventure. We cannot just stay home for fear of what might happen if we venture out. Well, we can, but it's no way to live. The need is to get going and see as much of the world as we can, whilst there's still time, 'cities of men, and manners', and to keep going, for as long as we may, and at the end there will always be the splendid things we missed.

I had gone to Venice the 'hard way', and it proved to be not hard at all; I had returned from it the hard way and it proved to be exhausting, but you have to leave home to experience the pleasure of returning to it – to the familiar things, your own kind of food, your own dear bed. . . .

Letting myself into Oak Cottage that October evening it was mission-accomplished so far as the Italian journey was concerned; it had all been very worth-while, despite exhaustion and loneliness; I had seen many beautiful and interesting places and things. All I had to do now was to write the book.

INDEX

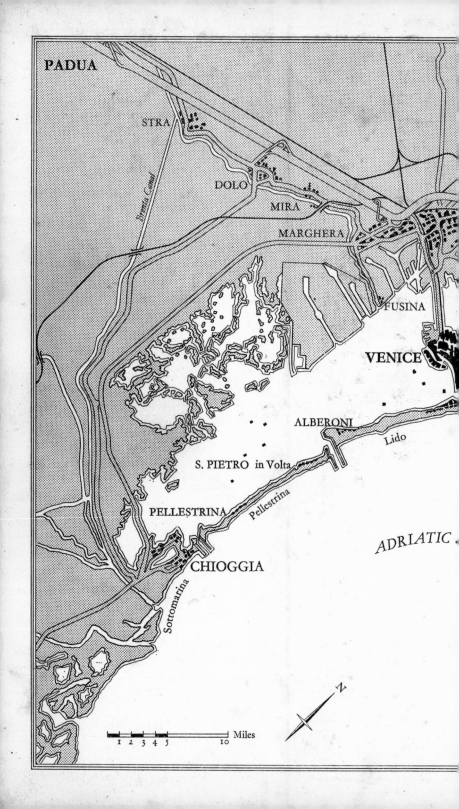